A GRAND ADVENTURE

America's First
Transcontinental Truck Run

GEORGE MACLEAN, ANTON WESTGARD, AND ARTHUR THOMPSON
WITH THE PIONEER FREIGHTER IN LOS ANGELES.

AMERICA'S FIRST TRANSCONTINENTAL TRUCK RUN

1911   2011

A GRAND ADVENTURE

RON CORBETT

GSPH

GENERAL STORE PUBLISHING HOUSE
499 O'Brien Road, Box 415
Renfrew, Ontario, Canada K7V 4A6
Telephone 1.613.432.7697 or 1.800.465.6072
www.gsph.com

ISBN 978-1-897508-90-9

Cover art, design, formatting: Magdalene Carson
Printed by Custom Printers of Renfrew Ltd., Renfrew, Ontario
Printed and bound in Canada

The author and publisher have made every attempt to locate
the sources of photographs and written excerpts.

Library and Archives Canada Cataloguing in Publication
Corbett, Ron, 1959-
    A grand adventure : America's first transcontinental truck run
/ Ron Corbett.
ISBN 978-1-897508-90-9
    1. Truck driving--United States--History. 2. Trucks--Routes--United States--
History. 3. Trucking--United States--History. 4. Mack trucks--History. 5. Saurer
trucks--History.   I. Title.
HE5623.C333 2011   388.3'240973   C2010-903708-1

All photos courtesy of the Mack Trucks Historical Museum unless otherwise noted.

Front cover: Making a road through New Mexico.
Back cover: Crossing the Continental Divide.

For Jack Mack

TRUCKIN' DOWN AN AMERICAN HIGHWAY IN THE SUMMER OF 1911.

Contents

Acknowledgements

The researching and writing of this book was its own journey. It began in the summer of 2008 as I was writing a series of newspaper stories about a timber crib making its way down the Ottawa River, the first time such a thing had been attempted in one hundred years.

When I returned home, I discovered an e-mail awaiting me from a woman named Rowena Stickler. Ms. Stickler said she had a "crazy old uncle," who had made the final timber-crib journey one hundred years before. In the same e-mail, she mentioned that she had another family member, a man from Campbell's Bay, who was the first person to drive a truck across the United States.

That's how this book began. In very short order, I was able to confirm Rowena's story. George MacLean had indeed driven a truck across the continental United States in 1911. The Mack Trucks Historical Museum of Allentown, Pennsylvania, even had photographs from the journey.

It was a promising beginning, but almost immediately, there were problems. While the museum had some lovely photographs, it had little in the way of source materials. There was no trip journal in other words. Not even an itinerary.

In those early days, what archival material I could find only added to my problems. MacLean started his trip in Denver, passed through Los Angeles and San Francisco, and ended up in New York City—that was all I was able to confirm. (There were even four published dates for when he began the journey.)

Thus began a lengthy research project that was both exhilarating (on those days when a date or fact was confirmed) and frustrating (the writing of this book began before I was even able to confirm who made the entire trip).

A great many people helped me solve these riddles, and I owe a debt of thanks to each of them. These include archivist, Tom Loetzbeier, and curator, Don Schumaker, of the Mack Trucks Historical Museum; Carrie Pruit, Gina Tecos, and John Gibson of the Detroit Public Library, National Automotive History Collection; Kim Bravo of the Automotive Reference Collection, Free Library of Philadelphia; Brian Silcoff of the Ottawa Public Library; Doug Hecox of the United States Department of Transportation; and David Pfeiffer of the United States National Archives at College Park.

The American Automobile Association

was a tremendous help, not only for sending me a copy of *Paving the Way*, a documentary by Depth of Field Productions that it co-sponsored, but also for employing Mike Camarano, a cartographer and archivist of great humour and common sense. Heather Hunter of the AAA also needs to be thanked, as do Dave Meier of the Iowa 80 Group and Lee Young of the American Truck Historical Society.

Closer to home, I wish to thank my editor, Beverley Humphries, who improved this story with each suggestion (a rare editorial skill), and Magdalene Carson, who did such a beautiful job designing the book. Finally, I would like to thank Tim Gordon, publisher of General Store Publishing House, who fell in love with this story the first time he heard it.

Prologue

In the summer of 1919, the American War Department dispatched a convoy of trucks from Washington, D.C., to San Francisco to complete a mission that could be summed up in a short sentence: Make your way west in all good speed.

The United States government was anxious to see how long it would take a convoy of motorized cargo vehicles—trucks, as most people had started to call them—to reach California. The country had just fought the Great War and military concerns—the safe and timely transportation of troops and supplies, in particular—was still very much on the minds of the nation's leaders.

That first motorized military convoy was under the command of Lt. Col. Charles W. McClure, who departed Washington with 24 officers, 15 War Department staff observers, 258 soldiers, and 81 motorized vehicles, the vast majority of them being trucks. The convoy left Washington on July 7, 1919.

It barely reached San Francisco. Indeed, nine of the trucks never did reach the West Coast, abandoned as junk along the way because they were so badly damaged (although the Firestone Tire Company did lend the army two of its own trucks when the convoy passed through Columbus, Ohio). Thus, the final tally for the mission was seven trucks missing in action.

The soldiers had to drive through swamps, mud-filled arroyos, and boulder-strewn switchbacks; they bogged down in the mud fields of Nebraska, were nearly swept away while fording rivers in Nevada, and struggled mightily to clear the peaks of the Rocky Mountains. Often the soldiers were forced to make their own roads as they travelled. Pick ax and shovel work. A lot of pick ax and shovel work whenever the trucks wouldn't fit through a narrow mountain pass, or a new path had to be cleared around an unmarked mud field or patch of quicksand.

The weather conspired against the convoy as well. The soldiers marched through snowstorms, hail storms, and dust storms. One day, it would be scorching hot; the next day, there would be a night so frigid they awoke with ice in their hair. The men ate field rations. Slept on the ground. Except for the lack of combat, it was combat conditions.

Among the soldiers who made that legendary trek across the United States was a young graduate from West Point. His name was Dwight D. Eisenhower, and he would later write of that 1919 trip:

In Illinois [the convoy] started on dirt roads, and practically no more pavement was encountered until reaching California. . . . two days were lost in the western part of Nebraska due to bad, sandy roads. From Orr's Ranch, Utah, to Carson City, Nevada, the road is one succession of dust, ruts, pits, and holes. This stretch was not improved in any way, and consisted only of a track across the desert. At many points on the road, water is twenty miles distant, and parts of the road are ninety miles from the nearest railroad.

Tough going, in other words. Tough even for a man who would have some passing acquaintance with such a thing during his life.

The 1919 military convoy became the subject of books and a prize-winning documentary. Years later, it helped convince Eisenhower to sign into law the Federal Aid Highway Act of 1956, which created America's interstate highway system. The story of that truck trip, thanks to the future thirty-fourth president of the United States, became well known. Not many, however, realize that the first truck trip across the United States actually took place eight years earlier. Without government help. Without a military supply line. Without a brigade of men and muscle. Indeed, that first truck trip was made by two men, driving a single truck.

Driving a truck across the continental United States in 1911, with really no roads to speak of in most of America's western states and territories, was the idea of the Saurer Motor Truck Company, which was soon to become part of the Mack Trucks Company. Saurer was a Swiss company that had opened an American sales office in New York City in 1908, followed by a manufacturing plant in Plainfield, New Jersey. The company's trucks had performed well in endurance and speed tests in Europe, with a record of fifty-three first-place showings.

Saurer wanted similar bragging rights in North America, but there were no national truck races to speak of at the time. So the company came up with its own test—take one of its new, four-and-a-half-ton, four-cylinder trucks and drive it across the United States, ocean to ocean.

The truck would travel with a payload: four tons of lumber, provisions, and camping equipment. Eight-and-a-half tons total travelling weight. This would show that there was a purpose to what they were doing. That a motorized cargo wagon could do the work of several mule teams. That it was a work vehicle for the new century.

Sometime during the planning of this promotional jaunt, it was pointed out to the Swiss executives that completing such a trip was not a given. Indeed, it might not work at all. The American Southwest was not the countryside of France or Germany. There would be no tolerance for error. If an axle broke in the middle of the desert, or if the truck rolled as it was coming down a switchback in Arizona, well, the ensuing publicity might not be the kind the company was seeking.

The Swiss auto executives thought this was an excellent observation and so decided to start the journey not with great fanfare in New York or Los Angeles but to steal away at the approximate halfway point in Denver. In this way, the most challenging part of the journey—the western leg, where there were only settlement trails through the deserts and over the mountains—would be attempted first. A failure at this stage would not be overly embarrassing. It might not even be reported.

The company checked its bet, in other words. The men running Saurer were about to attempt something so implausible and absurd, it seemed foolhardy to not only casual observers but to them as well.

The company hired as its driver George A. MacLean, originally from Campbell's Bay, Quebec, although he was living in New York City in 1911, doing occasional jobs for Saurer as a mechanic and demonstration driver. He had learned to drive the Swiss trucks while working for the T. Eaton Company of Toronto. MacLean was twenty-seven years old when he was hired, and MacLean family lore has it that he was not even told what he would be doing when his Swiss employers dispatched

him from New York City to Denver in the spring of 1911.

The other man who made the entire trip was Arthur C. Thompson, son of the man who held the Saurer sales and distribution rights in Illinois. Also a young man in his twenties, Thompson hailed from Chicago and was the Saurer Motor Truck Company's official representative for the journey.

As the two young men drove across the United States, they had companions, people who would drop in and out for different legs of the journey. There were executives from Saurer; journalists (both local and those working for the new automotive magazines); hired hands, Indians, representatives from local motoring clubs, and farmers (the farmers sometimes sticking around for a day or two out of curiosity after pulling the truck from a sinkhole).

The most notable of the travelling companions was A.L. Westgard, the man Saurer hired to be the "pilot" for the western leg of the journey. A self-described pathfinder, Westgard spent many years working for the American Automobile Association, mapping motor routes that would became part of Route 66 and the Lincoln Highway, among others. During the journey, he also did work for the Office of Public Roads, the forerunner to the United States' Department of Highways, which often commissioned a report from Westgard whenever he undertook a transcontinental journey.

It was a quixotic journey that MacLean and Thompson undertook in the spring and summer of 1911, a trip taken against the backdrop of a country about to change forever. This was an era of colourful characters imbued with can-do pioneer spirit: men like Carl Fisher, Jack Mack, and Cannonball Baker, some of the early pioneers of America's golden age of motoring, each of whom had a connection to the Saurer transcontinental truck run.

It was a good year, 1911, when you look back from the vantage point of one hundred years down the road. In 1911, Thomas Edison and Alexander Graham Bell were still tinkering in their laboratories; "What will they think of next?" was a commonly heard phrase on the streets of America. People were encouraged to dream big, go forth and mix things up, stretch limbs, look for new vistas, new cities, and new roads to travel. The Saurer-Mack truck trip across the United States was perfect for the times. It was an audacious trip that had so many difficulties lurking around the next bend or over the next hill, that anyone with a feint heart would never have set forth. Anyone with a practical bend of mind would have spent the rest of their lives planning it.

The truck that actually made the trip was called the Pioneer Freighter, a four-cylinder, thirty-seven-horsepower, open-bed truck that looked like a covered wagon because canvas tarps had been erected over the bed. The truck carried a large sign that read: Saurer Motor Truck, Ocean to Ocean, Pioneer Freighter.

If there were a road trip more different than the military convoy of eight years later, it would be hard to imagine. This was a crazy, shouldn't-have-worked-but-somehow-did road trip that would have been worthy of men like Teddy Roosevelt and Thomas Edison.

What follows is a re-creation of that trip. All dates, names, and mileages are actual. The photos were taken by A.L. Westgard and other photographers who accompanied George MacLean and Arthur Thompson on their trip.

Some of the conversations and thoughts are imagined, but that tends to happen a lot on a road trip. You dream. You aspire. You change plans.

And every once in a while, you make history.

POST CARD

Margaret,

Suppose this will surprise you, as you haven't heard from me for so long a time. Well, here's a map that might interest you a little. I am in Denver, marked x on the map, and will be leaving here Saturday morning with a big Saurer motor truck with about four tons load on it, going to drive it south through the desert and over the mountains to Los Angeles and San Francisco. . . . It is one of the most strenuous and hardest trips ever undertaken with a motor truck and if I can take that truck through we won't soon be forgotten by the Saurer Motor Truck Co. . . . If you feel like it, you may send me a note to Phoenix, Arizona, general delivery.

GEORGE MACLEAN, POSTCARD TO HIS FUTURE WIFE, MARCH 2, 1911

THE PIONEER FREIGHTER, SOMEWHERE IN THE AMERICAN SOUTHWEST.

Meeting a Pathfinder

My name is George MacLean. In 1910, I started working for the Saurer Truck Company, which is basically the Mack Truck Company. The two companies came together in 1911, dropped the name Saurer and chose to go with Mack instead, which I guess sounded better.

I came to the job by way of the T. Eaton Company in Toronto. I worked for a spell as a delivery driver on the department store's new horseless carriages before I started spending a lot of time in the livery after work, tinkering with the metal parts and the combustible engines, just trying to keep the things on the road. The T. Eaton Company was using Saurer trucks, and it wasn't long before one of the Saurer representatives contacted me about moving to New York to work for them. There I did mostly mechanical stuff although they asked me to drive sometimes to trade fairs and expositions and the like. The man I worked for most of the time was Mr. Otto, who lived in New Jersey and was helping set up the company's factory in Plainfield.

In the spring of 1911, Mr. Otto told me to take a train to Denver, Colorado, and check into the Brown Palace Hotel. There, I was to await a gentleman named A.L. Westgard, who would present himself. I was told to pack a steamer trunk as I might be gone from New York for a while. Mr. Otto didn't tell me much more than that, other than I should be in Denver by the start of the following week.

It was April 29 when I checked into the Brown Palace Hotel. I waited three days, reading in my room for the most part, going down to the dining room for my meals, and taking one trip to a nearby casino. There I lost five dollars and felt so guilty about it, I didn't bother going again. It was early evening on the third day when I finally got a knock on my door.

I opened it, and standing there was a short man dressed in knee-high leather boots, grey trench coat, and leather gloves (gauntlets he called them later) that he kept slapping in his hands. He had a full moustache and a thin goatee and reminded me of a poster I had seen once of Buffalo Bill Cody.

"Mr. MacLean?" he asked, and when I

answered, yes, he said, "A.L. Westgard. May I come in?"

I invited him in. He walked straight to the centre of my room where he started pacing in a circle before speaking. When he finally did, it seemed that I should pay attention to him. I closed the door and stood where I was.

"The truck will be arriving tomorrow, Mr. MacLean. It is a four-cylinder, thirty-seven-horsepower Saurer Pioneer Freighter. I have been told you know how to drive and maintain such a truck. If this is not the case, it is best you tell me now."

I told him I knew the truck.

"Very good. We will be leaving at first light in two days time. You should meet me at the rail yard tomorrow morning at ten to begin your inspection. The Saurer Motor Truck Company has made arrangements for our supplies. Do you have any questions?"

As I said, Mr. Otto hadn't told me much in New York, other than to report for my next assignment in Denver. I stood there thinking about it for a minute then decided I did have a question or two.

"What will we be doing with the truck?" I asked.

"They haven't told you?"

"No."

"Well, Mr. MacLean, you will be driving the Saurer, four-cylinder, thirty-seven-horse-power Pioneer Freighter across these glorious states of ours. Ocean to ocean."

"Across the United States?"

"Yes, Mr. MacLean, a transcontinental truck trip. It should be a grand adventure."

I didn't know what to say for a moment but finally managed to stammer: "Who all will be going?"

"Well, there will be yourself, Mr. MacLean. A hired hand that I understand will meet us at the train yard tomorrow. A representative from the Saurer Motor Truck Company. And myself, of course. I shall be your pathfinder."

He asked if I had any further questions. If he had stuck around for any length of time, I'm sure I would have had plenty. As there was already a lot to take in, I said no. He said goodbye shortly after that.

When Mr. Westgard left, I stood where I was for a long time, thinking about what he had just said. Keeping the new horseless carriages on the streets of Toronto and New York was a challenge. Taking one across the United States where I didn't believe there were any roads at all past Denver, well, I had trouble imagining it.

Then when I had thought about it long enough, I grabbed my coat and went to the front desk of the Brown Palace Hotel. I needed to buy some postcards. This was about to be the craziest thing I had ever done.

An Argument with a Purser

The next day, I got to the rail yards precisely at 10 a.m. and saw Mr. Westgard waiting for me. He was looking at his pocket watch and didn't seem happy.

"Mr. MacLean," he said when I reached him, "you have not left yourself much time. I thought a man in your profession would want to be here early to prepare for his inspection."

I looked at him in surprise, then quickly passed my hand over my face to conceal it. What exactly could I do before the train arrived? Without a truck to inspect there wouldn't be much of an inspection.

"Well, Mr. Westgard, I thought . . . I thought it best if I arrived at the time you requested."

Now it was his turn to look surprised as if he had just been rebuked. I immediately became worried about this. I hadn't meant anything by it. I just didn't understand why I should be there any earlier than the train.

"Yes, well, no harm done, I suppose. It just seems a surprise—a man in your profession and all. Myself, I have been here for nearly an hour."

I stood on the railway platform and didn't say anything. I always figure it is best to say nothing when you're around things that make no sense.

As we waited for the train to arrive, I looked around the station, noticing it was a lot bigger than the one in Toronto even though it had the same name—Union Station—like there were only so many things you could call a train station. I tried to remember what the station in Chicago had been called because I had transferred there, and it was bigger than either Denver or Toronto, but I couldn't recall. I wondered if it was another Union Station.

I had cut through the station proper on my way to meet Mr. Westgard out back on the railway sidings where you received cargo and freight that had been forwarded to you. There were trains hooting and clanging everywhere I looked, the steam so thick it was like an early morning fog. Mr. Westgard said the truck would be arriving on a Chicago, Rock Island and Pacific coming from Chicago, so we stood in silence on the platform waiting for one to arrive, staring down the tracks with the sun strong in our eyes.

General Mechanical Description
Saurer 4½-Ton Truck

Frame. The two side members are of special rolled steel, channels reinforced by similar cross-members. The frame depth is uniformly maintained from end to end throughout its whole length.

As a Road Sprinkler in Europe

Axles. Axles, both front and rear, are made of a special drop-forged steel of the highest quality and are of rectangular section.

Springs. The springs, both front and rear, are semi-elliptic in form. The spring-shackles are fitted with grease cups to afford proper lubrication.

Motor. The motor is of the four-cylinder, four-cycle, water-cooled type, with T-head type cylinders cast in pairs; inlet and exhaust valves located on opposite sides of motor, and each side operated by its separate cam-shaft. The inlet and exhaust valves are interchangeable and made of nickel-steel. Special care has been given to equilibrating the motor with the result that it runs silently.

Motor-shafts. The crank-shaft, cam-shafts, and fan-shaft are mounted on high-grade annular ball bearings of very large diameter. All shafts are of the finest grade of chrome-nickel steel.

Lubrication. The motor-lubricating system is of the forced-feed type, operated by a pressure pump driven from the pump-shaft. The pump forces oil into each of the four crank-chambers and maintains a given level. The connecting-rods are provided with scoops, which throw the oil to all portions of the crank-case.

Ignition. Ignition is by high-tension magneto. Special feature: the magneto is fixed to the moment of greatest induction, which point is advanced or retarded in relation to the piston by means of a helical sleeve. No weak sparks and, therefore, proper ignition and easy starting.

Cooling System. The cooling system consists of a honeycomb type radiator of a very efficient design, through which water is circulated by means of a centrifugal pump. A large fan placed directly behind the radiator efficiently supplements the radiator. The clutch-cone is provided with fan-shaped arms which assist in removing the heat.

Transmission. The transmission is of the selective, sliding-gear type, with four speeds forward and one reverse. The

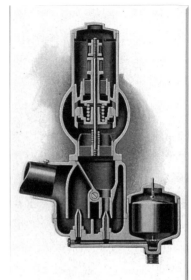

The Saurer Economy Carburetor

Saurer Brewery Truck in Europe

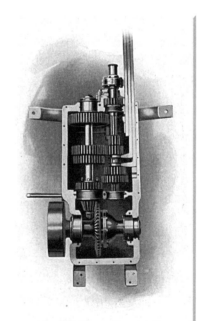

The Saurer Transmission

DETAILS FROM A 1912 SAURER SALES BROCHURE.

Rear View Saurer 4½-ton Chassis

The Saurer Motor

We both saw the plume of smoke at the same time even though it took quite a while before we heard the train. We watched the smoke trail get larger and larger then finally heard a far-away whistle. A few seconds after that the train took shape, the black lines gradually becoming more defined as though the train were being painted onto the horizon. By the time it reached the platform, the noise echoing off the mountains was almost deafening and ten minutes had passed since we saw the first trace of smoke against the sky. Mr. Westgard seemed pretty impatient by this time and marched straight toward a disembarking engineer. He demanded to know where the Saurer Pioneer Freighter was located, mentioning, as he enquired—and only for the engineer's benefit and prospects of future advancement in his career—that the train was fifteen minutes late.

The engineer knew exactly what Mr. Westgard was talking about. Which surprised me. It was a long train.

"Sure, I helped load her myself. Let me show you the car. It's called a truck, right?"

With that, we marched down the rails as the engineer counted off the cars, mumbling not so silently under his breath. We stopped when he mumbled twenty-two. Stopping directly in front of this railcar, he waved at a couple of roustabouts, who heaved open the large wooden doors. The engineer walked away, saying he would send over the purser.

The doors slid back on heavy metal grooves. Sunlight slit through the wooden slats of the railcar while two pigeons flew away in haste. Standing there waiting for us was the truck.

"Mr. MacLean," said Mr. Westgard. "I believe you can begin your inspection."

The truck wasn't new. I saw that right away. There was some wear on the tires, and one of the steel Prest-O-Lites had a slight dent in it. I found out later that she was a demonstration model, from the Saurer offices in Chicago. Still, it was a fine looking vehicle. Similar to what the T. Eaton Company had been using.

The frame was rolled steel, reinforced by cross members. The axles were made of galvanized steel, and the springs had grease cups, which I told myself as I bent over to begin my inspection, I would have to remember to keep filled. The motor was water cooled, with four T-shaped cylinders cast in pairs. The inlet and exhaust valves were on opposite sides of the motor, each side operated by a separate camshaft. The valves looked to be made of nickel steel, which made sense.

The ball bearings for the various shafts were quite large although that was a feature of Saurer trucks I was familiar with. It helped smooth out the ride although it made getting spare parts difficult from time to time. I hoped Mr. Westgard had thought about that. The ignition was a high-tension magneto, with a sleeve connecting it to the pistons. I was pleased to see our truck would start all right, no matter what the weather. The radiator was a honeycomb type, which, for my money, was the best kind on the market. I was pleased to see that as well.

The transmission had four forward speeds and one reverse. The same large ball bearings were carrying the gear shafts. There was a cone-shaped clutch with leather over a rubber ring and three kinds of brakes: one for the differential, an emergency brake that could be operated with a foot pedal, and another one that I had never seen before, attached to a throttle-lever on the steering wheel. That brake wasn't on the Saurers I drove back home. The lever advanced the exhaust camshaft. I thought it through and realized that it must convert the motor into a two-cycle air-compressor, which meant that you must be able to keep the clutch engaged when you put on the brakes. Good heavens.

As I was inspecting the truck, a purser arrived. Before he could open his mouth, Mr. Westgard said:

"My dear man, this truck has not been blocked and tied properly."

He pointed with scorn to a wooden block lying in the corner of the railcar.

"That piece of wood there, sir?" answered the purser. "You be talkin' 'bout that piece of wood there?"

"Yes, that block of wood. Is there another loose block you see in the car?"

"No, sir. That be the only one. And has your vehicle moved in any way?"

"I'm not sure if she has. That hardly seems the point. If the job had been done properly there would not be a loose block in the car, potentially flying around to hit people and property. That would seem to be rather the point."

"Ah, yes. And was there any damage, sir? To either people or property?"

"I hope for your sake there has not. Mr. MacLean!"

I looked up from what I was doing, which was mostly hiding my face from the purser. Maybe one block had been kicked free, but I didn't think the other three had moved so much as an inch on the run down from Chicago.

"Mr. MacLean, has the Pioneer Freighter been damaged as a result of the shoddy workmanship performed by the Chicago, Rock Island and Pacific Railroad?"

"The truck looks fine, Mr. Westgard. Don't think she ever moved."

"Yes, well, a fortunate turn of events. It seems the Good Lord has been looking out for us."

"So, no damage, sir?" asked the purser.

"It appears not."

"Yes, well then, if you can just sign here to show you are in receipt of your merchandise, I'll be on my way."

"In the future," said Mr. Westgard as he took the waybill, "you should teach your men how to properly block and tie a modern vehicle for transport in one of your railcars."

"Yes, well, roustabouts aren't the people I deal with normally, sir. It's right there—the line on the bottom right."

Mr. Westgard looked appalled as the man reached across his chest and pointed to a line on the waybill.

"The Office of Public Roads will expect better service from Chicago, Rock Island and Pacific Railroad in the future," said Mr. Westgard as he signed the bill and handed it back, letting the purser know he was still angry. "Much better service."

"Quite right, sir. Well, if there's nothing more, I'll be on my way. If I see a roustabout, I'll send him in your direction."

The purser turned and waddled away, a rolling penguin kind of a walk. He seemed like a happy man.

"Mr. MacLean," said Mr. Westgard, turning to look at me, clearly a little miffed. "Does the truck meet with your approval?"

"It's a fine truck," I answered quickly. "It's not new: There is a bit of wear on the tires, and there's a dent, right here in the Prest-O-Lite, but it seems in tip-top shape. It comes with air brakes?"

"Yes, one of the newest features on the Saurer trucks. It should make the driving easier."

"I'll say. You should be able to use the brakes while still in gear."

"Precisely. Has anything else caught your attention during the inspection?"

"Well, these trucks have some special parts that other trucks don't have. The ball bearings, for example, are much larger than what most trucks use. Will we be travelling with spare parts?"

"Very good question, Mr. MacLean. I shall be meeting the representative of the Saurer Motor Truck Company this evening for dinner: a Mr. Thompson. I have been told he has brought spare parts. Ball bearings? Is this what you wish me to inquire of Mr. Thompson?"

"Yes."

"Very well. Anything else?"

I stood there for a minute trying to think if there was anything else. Truck looked good. Bring ball bearings. That about covered it. Mr. Westgard looked at me with a look of such anticipation, however, I felt compelled to say more.

"As I said, it's a fine looking truck. They certainly haven't sent us a clunker."

"I would think not, Mr. MacLean. The Saurer Motor Truck Company has high hopes for our little adventure. As does the Office of Public Roads and, I would suspect, the entire Good Roads Movement."

"Well, it's a mighty fine looking truck," I said again.

"And, in your opinion, is she up to the task before her now of transporting us to Los Angeles, then on to New York?"

I looked at the truck, not wanting to look directly at Mr. Westgard and annoy him. To Los Angeles? Maybe it can make deliveries around Denver, impress all the local liveries and department stores. But Los Angeles? Not wanting the silence to drag on too long and not being able to think of anything else, I said:

"Are there roads to Los Angeles?"

"Well, the trails that opened up the West are certainly still there, Mr. MacLean. They have worked nicely for a generation or two. Do you see a problem with us taking a horseless carriage down these trails, considering, after all, that we shall be using a superior mode of transportation?"

"No, I guess not. If you know the way."

"I most certainly do, Mr. MacLean. I mapped the way from Denver to Los Angeles for the Touring Club of America just last year."

I tried my best to look impressed although I wasn't really sure what he meant by mapping the way from Denver to Los Angeles. Just then, a man in a cloth cap, wearing a heavy-knit sweater and carrying a well-worn leather satchel, came running down the railway siding. He was portly. Sweating profusely. Looked around my age.

"Ah," said Mr. Westgard. "If I am correct, the final member of our road crew has arrived."

Canadian Whisky

"**S**orry I'm late," panted the man when he reached us. "I was directed to the wrong siding when I arrived."

Mr. Westgard shook the man's hand and looked at him carefully. He didn't say anything for a few seconds as if he were mentally judging the likelihood of that story. Finally, he spoke: "Mr. Grey, we will be leaving from the garage next to the Brown Palace Hotel tomorrow morning precisely at seven. Do you anticipate any difficulties?"

"No sir, no sir," the man said as the satchel in his sweaty hand slipped out of his grasp and fell to the ground, where he ignored it. "There won't be any problems tomorrow. It was a smart idea coming to Union Station today, so I could meet you and have a look at the truck."

That was the right thing to say: Mr. Westgard's chest noticeably increased in circumference.

"Yes, well, our inspection is concluded. It appears we are ready for departure."

He looked at the Saurer truck. The last of the wooden blocks was being kicked away from the wheels by a mean-looking roustabout, who didn't seem to like our company much. Mr. Westgard didn't seem to even notice him. Two other roustabouts were moving a wooden ramp into position, so the truck could be driven off the railcar.

"What do you think of her, Mr. Grey?"

Grey looked at the truck. Looked over at me. Kept his gaze on me for a minute. Then said:

"I think she looks lovely."

This time Mr. Westgard's chest looked like it was going to start popping off the medallions and pins affixed to his coat.

"Yes, I think she looks lovely as well. Although perhaps in need of some minor alterations. Well, gentlemen, I have business I must attend to. Mr. MacLean, if you would be so kind as to drive the truck to the garage, I shall meet you there tomorrow morning."

With that he turned and strode away, leaving Grey and me to stare at his back as it retreated through the steam of Union Station.

Later that night at the Brown Palace Hotel, Howard Grey ("Just call me Howie. Everyone does.") and I got acquainted over a bottle of Canadian rye whiskey I had brought down for the trip. I had not known exactly when I would drink it, but that night seemed about right.

"To Los Angeles. And then to New York?" Howie was lying on my bed, laughing and saying over and over again the words that had made him laugh steadily for the past five minutes: "To Los Angeles. And then to New York?"

This time I laughed, too.

"That's what he says. Sweet Jesus, I work for the truck company. I have to go. Where did you come from?"

Grey was continuing to kill himself laughing.

"Some fellow named Thompson hired me the other night at the casino. He heard me talking about fixing an old Black Crow touring car my uncle left me and wanted to know if I was any good with my hands. I told him I was the best mechanic in Denver.

"Then he said he was going on a truck trip, and would I be interested in coming along? Said they already had a driver who was pretty good with his hands, but one more mechanic never hurts."

"That was it?" I asked. "He didn't tell you anything else? Didn't tell you how long you would be gone for?"

"You know, I didn't really ask."

We were killing ourselves. Absolutely killing ourselves. There is nothing better in the world than Canadian whiskey.

"I BELIEVE THEY LIKE THE SIGN."

Saurer Motor Truck, Ocean-to-Ocean, Pioneer Freighter

The next morning, bright and early, I was in the garage next to the Brown Palace Hotel, staring in embarrassment at the truck. Mr. Westgard must have kept a printer up most of the night. There was now a canvas tarp over the bed of the truck, and on one side of the tarp was a large sign that read: "Saurer Motor Truck, Ocean-to-Ocean, Pioneer Freighter."

The sign was above three other signs for Goodrich Tires.

I stared at the truck and thought of a circus vehicle, the kind that used to roll into Campbell's Bay every summer to set up tents and then sell tickets to see bearded women and monkey boys.

"Nothing wrong with some promotion as we set forth on our little adventure—right, gentlemen?" said Mr. Westgard, who was dressed like Teddy Roosevelt that morning: leather boots that rose to his knees, khaki jacket with a pleated tail, thick canvas pants that bunched out like pantaloons from the mouth of his boots.

Next to him stood a man in similar Teddy Roosevelt gear, although he was much taller and broader-shouldered than Mr. Westgard and also about twenty years younger. He had slicked-back blonde hair and a clean-shaven face.

"Looks wonderful, Boss," said Howie although I knew he was slightly the worse for wear that morning. The garish signs must have been giving him a headache.

"Yes, it will be wonderful letting everyone we meet know immediately what the horseless carriage, modified for trade and commerce, is capable of doing. A noble message, gentlemen; a noble message we will be spreading across these glorious states of ours."

Most of this was addressed to the younger man standing next to Mr. Westgard, who gave a shy smile, nodded his head but didn't speak. Either he was hung over like Howie or just as embarrassed as me.

"Mr. MacLean, Mr. Grey, allow me to introduce Mr. Arthur Thompson. Mr. Thompson is from Chicago. His father holds the distribution rights for the Saurer Motor Truck

Company in Illinois. He shall be accompanying us to Los Angeles."

The man stepped forward and shook our hands. It was a firm, friendly grip, and although I couldn't be completely sure—maybe he had some sort of facial tick—he seemed to give me a slight wink.

"Well, we have some work to do before we depart," said Mr. Westgard. "Mr. Grey, in that crate over there"—he pointed to a wooden crate next to the truck—"you shall find the spare parts. They shall have to be inspected and loaded.

"Mr. MacLean, against the wall over there"—again he pointed—"you shall find the lumber we are bringing. The remainder of the provisions are next to the lumber. These will need to be inspected and loaded as well.

"Mr. Thompson"—this time he turned but didn't point—"if you will accompany me to the bench over there, I think a quick survey of our maps is in order."

With everyone safely assigned a task (I was getting the impression our pilot would have instructed Moses himself on the proper way to carry stone tablets down a mountain), Mr. Westgard walked away. I dropped my satchel and looked around the garage.

It was early morning, but the garage, which was little more than an addition tacked on to the hotel livery, was already a blur of activity. There were stagecoaches getting rigged for the day's work, cowboys giving their horses a last rub-down before tossing saddle bags and sleeping bags on their flanks, and prosperous men in three-piece suits, standing near one of the front pens, smoking cigars, and laughing loudly. There was the smell of straw and manure and melting dew—a good early-morning smell I took up my nose for all it was worth.

After I finished sniffing around, I started checking the lumber and provisions, which is something I would have done anyway without Mr. Westgard telling me to. I had been on enough hunting trips in Campbell's Bay to know you can survive almost anything in the wilderness except the stupidity that makes you leave something important back home. We had four barrels of gasoline, a barrel of oil, and two barrels of water. There were tents, axes, camp saws, and a full galley's worth of pots, pans, tin plates, and tin cutlery. Two crates of food made up of flour, coffee, dried beans, and maize were packed in wet oilskin cloth, along with eggs, cheese, beef wrapped in butcher's paper, cans of pickles, beets, beans, and pork. There were also bed rolls, rifles, picks, shovels, what looked like honest-to-God Hudson's Bay blankets, and tools for the truck: the metal wrenches that were good at turning the parts. Hammers. Screwdrivers.

Next to all of this was stacked two tons of oak planking. I knew a bit about timber, coming from Campbell's Bay where there were timber runs down the Coulonge River and the Ottawa River. Every spring, many of the boys I went to school with got good jobs guiding the timber cribs to the mills down river. It was nice planking we were bringing. A shame what we were going to do to it.

While I was working, Howie inspected the crate of spare parts although it was a small crate, and I wondered what was taking him so long. I looked over from time to time, and it almost seemed like he was asleep: his body rocked unsteadily on his knees, and his eyes were closed, which seemed to me a funny way to inspect anything.

I finished loading the truck, gave Howie a nudge so he would start loading the spare parts, then went over to Mr. Westgard to announce we were ready to go.

"Everything has passed your inspection, Mr. MacLean?"

"Everything is right as rain. We're carrying a lot of gear. It takes up the entire bed. Can't think of anything we might be forgetting."

"Yes, I was impressed as well. We have Mr. Thompson's father to thank for that. He has done an admirable job of outfitting our little expedition."

Mr. Westgard looked over at Mr. Thompson, who almost seemed to blush, like he was embarrassed by the mention of his father and all the provisions he had set us up with.

"My father is not a man to do things in half measures, Mr. Westgard. I am somewhat surprised there is not a Pullman car accompanying us as well."

"Yes, well, a difficult thing to arrange, considering how far we will be from a rail line during much of our journey. All right, gentlemen, shall we?"

And with that we climbed into the Pioneer Freighter, me behind the wheel with Mr. Westgard sitting beside me, and Howie and Mr. Thompson in the back perched on the oak planking, which they had covered with the Hudson's Bay blankets to make it a little more tolerable. It was mid-morning of March 4, and as we drove out of the garage and made our way down Larimer Street, people waved at us. Mr. Westgard, who had spread one of his maps on his lap, looked up and waved back. Before turning his attention back to his maps, he said:

"I believe they like the sign."

Road Trips

Back in 1911, people didn't use the phrase "road trips." When you travelled any distance you were going on an excursion, or a trek; no one ever thought of combining the words road and trip. It was a long time before people started using the phrase, even though that journey with Mr. Westgard and Mr. Thompson — it was a road trip.

Years later, when I was back living in Campbell's Bay, I bought a set of Encyclopedia Britannicas from a man who came to my front door. I have always enjoyed reading — the newspapers from Ottawa; the automotive magazines from the States; books by Owen Wister and Zane Grey, who for my money was ten times more interesting than that Hemingway fellow who could write a good hunting story but went way too crazy for bull fighting, which never struck me as much of a sport.

In those Britannicas, I read that the first road trip was made by Ramses II, an Egyptian pharaoh who "came down on the Medeans in his chariot after driving all night from Memphis." Which made me laugh. Even though the "driving all night from Memphis" part

was pretty good, I had trouble believing this would have been the first road trip. Was there some sort of curfew in the days of Ramses II? Was this really the first overnight chariot run in all of what the Britannicas called "antiquity"?

It shows the problem, though, of trying to trace the history of road trips. Or trying to define them. Or stating with certainty what needs to happen in order to be going on the real deal instead of just pretending, the way a lot of people do whenever they drive even slightly farther than where they're accustomed to driving.

According to the Britannicas, there was a lot of chariot traffic in antiquity, and some of those trips might be what you call road trips. Alexander's march into India sounded like a road trip to me. Same for Hannibal taking those elephants over the Swiss Alps. Young rich kids in the days of Julius Caesar used to travel around Europe all the time — sometimes gone for months at a time — making their way down dusty roads, drinking too much wine and beer in Roman taverns every

HORATIO NELSON JACKSON, 1903, IN HIS WINTON, "THE VERMONT."
University of Vermont special collection

night, then getting up the next day to complain of sore heads and the kilometres that needed to be travelled before they could drink again. A classic college road trip.

So, maybe road trips started back then with hungover Romans and Egyptian pharaohs, but if you ask me, I'll tell you that road trips only started when people started driving automobiles and trucks. I think most people would agree with me.

Which would make the first road trip across the United States the one taken by Horatio Nelson Jackson. Jackson was a doctor from Vermont, who was in San Francisco in the spring of 1903 visiting some other doctors. His doctor friends took him out drinking one night to the San Francisco University Club;

he must have gotten pretty sloshed because before the night was over, he had made a fifty-dollar wager with a man who said horseless carriages would never be able to drive across the United States.

Strange thing was, Jackson made the bet even though he didn't own a car and had rarely driven one. He had nerve. I'll say that much for Horatio Nelson Jackson. The next day, when he was sober and probably could have weaseled out of the bet easily enough, he went out instead and bought a second-hand Winton Touring Car, some camping gear, a couple of pistols, and a shotgun, then hired an out-of-work chauffeur named Sewell Crocker and headed for New York City. The date was May 23.

Fifteen miles into the trip he blew a tire. He used the only spare he had to replace it and was never able to find another one that fit the car. Jackson spent the rest of the trip knowing his journey would be finished the moment he got another flat. But someone must have been looking out for him because he never did.

Mind you, he broke just about everything else on the car. They had to replace the headlights in California. The carburetor in Idaho. The wheel bearings in Wyoming. Somewhere in Idaho, Jackson and Sewell picked up a pit bull for a travelling companion, an animal they named Bud. The two men became quite fond of their dog, even giving the animal his own pair of travelling goggles. A photographer in Idaho took a photo of Bud sitting in the car wearing his goggles, and it ran in newspapers across the country. By the time they reached Cheyenne, the road crew in the second-hand Winton was famous, and crowds had started gathering along their route.

They reached New York City on July 26, sixty-two days after leaving San Francisco. There were throngs of people waiting for them in Times Square, including Horatio's wife, who had taken the train up from Vermont to congratulate her husband. They drove home in the second-hand Winton for one last road trip. In their laneway in Vermont, the drive shaft broke.

People started taking a lot of road trips after that. Six years later, a woman named Alice Ramsay piled into a green Maxwell 30 with three of her lady friends for their own transcontinental road trip from Hell's Gate in New York City to San Francisco Bay. None of the other women could drive a car. Only 152 miles of the trip were on paved roads.

The whole thing was a publicity stunt by the Maxwell Automotive Company, publicity stunts involving trying to do something crazy with an automobile or a truck being all the rage back then. Anyway, the housewife from Hackensack, New Jersey, beat Nelson's transcontinental run by three days, arriving just in time for a big party at the St. James Hotel in San Francisco after fifty-nine days on the road.

I read that both Jackson and Ramsay stayed motor enthusiasts their entire lives. Jackson even ran for governor of Vermont because people liked all the crazy things he did behind the wheel of an automobile (although they didn't like him well enough to actually elect him governor).

You'd think, perhaps, given the hardships in going any great distance in a car or truck back then—in taking any decent sort of road trip—they might have given up. Decided it was a mug's game. Abandoned the sport.

Surprisingly, they did the exact opposite. Like there was some reverse magnetism at play although I couldn't say with certainty how such a thing would work.

Looking at Maps
with a Talkative Pathfinder

Ten miles out of Denver, the road disappeared. That's one of the things I remember quite well about the trip: how as soon as we lost sight of Denver, we lost the macadamized roads as well.

In front of us, after that, was a trail marked with stone markers that Mr. Westgard had to use his spyglasses to see and then direct me toward. It's a good thing the markers were there because the trail seemed more fantasy than real; without the markers, I would have been looking at nothing more than a maze of arroyos and dry gulches, all intersecting and going in crazy circles.

In spite of the terrain we were travelling over, the constant need to slow down and check for markers, there were stretches on that first day when I managed to get the truck into third gear, and I was mighty impressed with that. The engine sounded powerful. The transmission never missed a shift. The tires were more than capable and didn't seem to mind bouncing off the rocks.

As I drove, Mr. Westgard showed me the route we would be taking to Los Angeles, etching it on a map spread across his lap. From Denver, we would travel south toward New Mexico, crossing over at a town called Trinidad. Once in New Mexico, we would pass through Las Vegas, Santa Fe, and Albuquerque. On nights when we couldn't reach a town, we would pitch a tent or try to reach a cattle or mining camp. Mr. Westgard had marked these camps on his map—the ones he thought we might stay at—and I started to memorize some of the names: Camp Mormon, Camp Trouble, Camp Golden Sunset.

(We were going to reach Camp Golden Sunset before we reached Camp Trouble, which seemed unfortunate and wrong-headed to me. Why would trouble come after a golden sunset? It should have been the other way around. But what can I say? I was a young man back then and didn't realize you spent a lot of your life wishing for reversals like that.)

Once we were rid of New Mexico, we would pass through Arizona, travelling through Clifton and Phoenix and a lot more mining camps and other places Mr. Westgard had marked on the map, which he explained were small Mexican villages that never made it to an official map.

During that stretch of the trip, we would cross the Rockies—through the White Mountains range—where, according to the map I was looking at, which had elevations marked in circular, squiggly lines (a topographical map, Mr. Westgard called it), we would be more than 10,000 feet above sea level.

From there—assuming we made it—we would cross a desert, the Sonoran Desert, where we would suddenly be at 200 feet below sea level. Which was a hell of a swing. After that, we would be on the homestretch in California, travelling through Indio, Palm Springs, then on to Riverside, Pomona, and finally Los Angeles.

"I call it the Trail to Sunset," said Mr. Westgard when he had finished showing me the route. "I am in negotiations right now with the American Automobile Association to have the route published as a map."

Mr. Westgard travelled with a fine collection of maps. He had topographical maps, city maps, and something he called "strip maps." As he was folding the maps and putting them away in his satchel, I asked how long it would take us to reach Los Angeles.

"Ah, Mr. MacLean," he said, stuffing away the last of the maps. "Paper can tell us only so much. What the Good Lord brings to us in the way of rain and mud, this will tell the rest of the story.

"If there is one thing I have learned as a pathfinder, it is surely that."

Which was his answer. I was hoping for something with a number attached to it, but I didn't get it, nor could I really complain. The man, after all, had mentioned God. So I sat there trying to guide the truck around the arroyos as best I could, thinking about weather and God and wondering what in the world I was getting myself into.

The countryside we were driving through was like nothing I had seen before, coming as I did from Quebec, where it was all forests and rivers. This was the edge of the Great Plains, with mountains to the west of us and strange rock formations—mesas, buttes—dotting the horizon in front. By midday, we were passing a large butte called Castle Rock, named because it looked like a castle, although I didn't really see that. Certainly, it was a large hunk of rock: it was big enough to cast a shadow over us as we passed well to the east of it.

As the day wore on, Mr. Westgard became quite talkative. This was not always the case, I came soon enough to learn, for the man had his moods. Some evenings, he would seem almost sad, saying very little around the cook fire and then retiring early to write a letter. Or read his Bible. Or count the beads on his rosary. On those nights, Mr. Thompson and I

A.L. WESTGARD AND ARTHUR THOMPSON MAKING CAMP ON THE ROAD OUT OF DENVER.

would often spy him lying in his bedroll with his eyes wide open, waiting to fall asleep.

"We'd best be quiet, George," Mr. Thompson would say on those nights. "Mr. Westgard is in one of his holy moods."

Then there were days when he would seem distracted or annoyed, like the day he read a magazine story about another pathfinder, a man named W.E. Williams who was proposing a transcontinental highway that would start in Cumberland, Maryland, and end at San Diego, California. Which didn't make sense to Mr. Westgard. There wasn't even an ocean in Cumberland. And the route

Williams was proposing—south instead of east, then around those damnable roads surrounding Atlanta—if you could call any of them a road, why it was absurd. The man was drunk. According to Mr. Westgard.

The rest of that day, Mr. Westgard was angered by little things. Muttered under his breath whenever we needed to jump the truck over a busted culvert or a rut. Didn't help out as much as he normally did.

So, the man had his moods. He certainly did. Although that first day, he was probably in the best mood of the trip. Maybe there is no secret to this, as the beginning of many things can often be the most pleasant. A fishing trip. Christmas Day. Courtship. The beginning of a road trip. It works that way for a lot of people, too. Every mile ahead had the potential to be a good mile. Every mile was something you had yet to experience. So Mr. Westgard was talkative that day, and when I asked him questions, he answered effusively and, it seemed to me, without guile.

He told me he had come to these "glorious states of ours" in 1883 as a young man from Norway, a country I knew nothing about. Mr. Westgard explained that it would probably be similar to stretches of Canada if you were to live by the sea with a fishing village nearby that had stone buildings and a church so old it sometimes scared you.

"I was hoping to be an engineer," he said. "I even attended university in New York City, although it was a costly enterprise, and I could not sustain it. I had to leave after one semester, which was a pity as my grades were exemplary.

"I moved around the country after that — Texas, Illinois — until I accepted a position as a surveyor for the Century Map Company of Philadelphia, Pennsylvania. In my capacity as a surveyor for this company, I had the opportunity to walk around these glorious states of ours pushing a trundle wheel."

"What's a trundle wheel?" asked Mr. Thompson.

"Well, it is a wheel of exactly one-yard circumference attached to a handle. I would walk behind the wheel, pushing it and counting the revolutions, so I could record distances.

"If you care to imagine it, Mr. Thompson, imagine a child's toy — a wheel attached to a push stick; now imagine a man walking the width and breadth of this country, every state east of the Rockies, pushing such a wheel. That man would have been me, gainfully employed for many years by the Century Map Company of Philadelphia, Pennsylvania. What do you think of that, gentlemen?"

Mr. Thompson seemed surprised by the quick question and didn't answer right away. Howie was sound asleep and never heard the question. I was concentrating hard on not driving the truck into an arroyo and so I didn't answer, either. The lack of an answer didn't slow Mr. Westgard down any, though, as he quickly resumed talking.

"Yes, it was a wonderful piece of equipment, the trundle wheel. It could record distance, longitude, and latitude. With this information, along with the other observations I obtained while on my daily walks — I would record every rural address, every barn, every trail I saw — then I would submit reports to my head office, which led to the publishing of the informative city directories and city maps for which the Century Map Company is still highly regarded to this day."

The path in front of me was clearing. I was switching into third gear, could hear Mr.

Thompson in the back ask: "Did you draw the maps?"

"No, that was a job given to others, although I am quite sure I could have matched the work that was finally produced with very little effort on my part.

"Competent. Make no mistake, it was competent. I don't want to give you the wrong impression. But it didn't have the smell of the country to it, if you know what I mean."

He fell silent for a minute, so Mr. Thompson could contemplate what he meant.

"Anyway, I never aspired to that sort of job. The mapmakers, the official ones, at least, sat in dreary offices in Philadelphia. I was quite happy doing what I was doing."

"Pushing a wheel?"

"Yes, Mr. Thompson. Pushing a wheel."

Looking back, I might have seen a surveyor before I met Mr. Westgard, even though I had never heard the word until he used it and can't say with certainty that's actually what I saw.

But I remember seeing a man walking through the forests near Campbell's Bay one summer's day, pushing a wheel through a dense clump of red pine. I had been fishing for trout on the Coulonge River at the time. It was getting close to mid-morning, although there was a dense fog that had yet to be burned away, and it felt earlier.

I looked up when I heard him. The steady clump, clump of feet through the forest with a mechanical thudding sound at the same time, a strange sound that was somehow rhythmic.

I looked up and there—framed by the branchless trunks of some red pine—was a young man wearing a leather skull cap and leather britches, pushing a large bicycle wheel through the trees. The fog swirled around his feet. Obscured the wheel as it dipped and rose. He was whistling and swatting away mosquitoes. Then he disappeared in the mist before I had time to get over my surprise and perhaps rise from my perch near the river and talk to him.

A few months later, several families moved to Campbell's Bay. They took up farming in the forests around the Coulonge River on what my father called "homesteading lots" although other days he called it "government land they're giving away to anyone stupid enough to take it."

The families spoke in languages none of us could understand. Seemed anxious to get homes built as soon as possible. Tried to grow corn and potatoes on land that was thin and cold until most of them gave up and tried other things. A lot of the boys that came to town in those years, I grew up with, and they made damn fine lumbermen.

"A wheel is always the first thing," Mr. Westgard told me on that first day. "If you think about it for a minute, you'll realize it's true. A wheel is always the first thing to arrive."

A Snowstorm at Palmer Lake

That first night, we reached Palmer Lake, about forty miles south of Denver. It was a beautiful lake, not so big you couldn't see the far shoreline but big enough to make you think there may be some good-sized lake trout in it. The foothills of the Rockies ringed the lake, and there was still snow on the ground where we parked the truck.

Howie started building a cook fire while Mr. Thompson and I took out the gear and food we would need for supper. This surprised me as I wasn't expecting any help. Being a driver for an automotive company—which I had been doing for the past year—was a lot like being a fishing guide back home. You travelled with well-to-do people dressed in fancy outdoor clothes ("sports" we called them when they weren't around to hear us), and when there was work to be done—fish to be cleaned, a tent to be pitched, a meal to be cooked—that was always the job of the guide. I couldn't remember a sport ever helping out.

But Mr. Thompson seemed more comfortable around me than he did around Mr. Westgard and he was always trying to help me.

"Look what we have here, George," he said when he took the butcher's paper off the meat we were carrying. I looked at what he was holding: thick slaps of Colorado beef cut into two-inch-thick strips, so thick the marbling looked like the rings of an old maple.

"My gosh, that's a nice piece of meat. How hungry are you, Mr. Thompson?"

"Hungry enough to eat half of this just by myself, George. I don't see the sense in saving any of it. Let's cook it all up tonight."

He wasn't going to get any argument from me and, as I got out the cast-iron skillets and the potatoes, Mr. Thompson said I could call him Arthur, which I never did, not even once. It wasn't that I had anything against the name; there are probably a lot of fine Arthurs in this world. But it never seemed right to me, calling a boss by his first name. It would have been like calling Mr. Otto by his first name, which I couldn't have done even if I wanted to because I had no idea what his first name might have been. Mr. Thompson was the Saurer Motor Truck Company representative on this demonstration journey, and it didn't matter if he

THERE WERE NO MOTELS IN 1911. CAMPING WAS PART OF ANY ROAD TRIP.

was younger than me. He was the boss. No different than Mr. Otto.

Still, Mr. Thompson was a great help most days. He even helped Howie get the fire started that first night after Howie said he didn't need the help.

"I'm fine, Arthur. I've been making cook fires my whole life," Howie protested.

"Yes, well, if we throw in some pine cones for kindling, I think it would be a little faster."

"Pine cones?"

After the fire was started, I cooked up the steaks, buried the potatoes in the embers of the fire, and cooked them up as well. We ate supper around the cook fire, all of us pretty tired and not talking much. Clumps of snow chilled the air around us, and you could just make out some foothills to the west, running in a long, crooked line, and looking, for all the world, like some big, fat piece of jewellery someone had thrown down. I slept well that night. Remember thinking that maybe we weren't going to have many problems at all.

Overnight it snowed. By morning, it had become a squall. I was the first one to awake, and after I got over my surprise, I threw off the bedroll and rushed to the firewood. Howie had forgotten to cover it. Stupid. Stupid. Stupid.

The rest of the crew woke up soon afterward and they were just as surprised as I was. Howie, in particular, who prided himself on being able to track weather patterns, was angry, saying this shouldn't be happening, the sky had been too clear the night before, the winds light, it never should have happened. Which struck me as a silly thing to say in the middle of a snowstorm, but he said it anyway.

The firewood wasn't that wet, which was a lucky break although we had to use one of the pieces of lumber from the truck for kindling. Once I got the fire started, Mr. Westgard said there was no sense heading out right away as we couldn't even see the trail markers for the snow.

"We shall have to stay here until it blows through," he said. "We will only make things worse if we try to leave."

My dad used to say the same thing about hunting; that if I ever got caught in an early-season snowstorm, I should find some shelter and hunker down until it ended. Don't even think about trying to make it home. Mr. Thompson and I accepted the news of being stranded without complaint, although Howie looked annoyed and stayed that way for several hours.

The storm lasted the rest of the day. It wasn't until mid-evening that it started to taper, the wind falling to a whisper, a few stars starting to show high above the clouds. Howie took all this as a good sign.

"We'll be back on the road first thing in the morning," he told us as if he were suddenly the pilot. "Mark my words. First thing in the morning."

First thing in the morning, we awoke to discover the temperature had spiked overnight, the snow had melted, and the ground around us had turned to mud. We were up to our knees in it. The truck was stuck solid in it.

"We shall need to wait until the ground freezes," said Mr. Westgard after he had inspected the truck. "If we're lucky, that will happen tonight."

We weren't lucky. It took two more nights before the temperature came back to normal, and we could finally get on our way, already three days behind schedule. Howie complained loudly that there had been some sort of witchcraft going on at Palmer Lake.

"Never should have happened," he said over and over again. "Stuff like that just don't happen unless a place is cursed, unless it has some sort of witch's curse on it or something like that."

Again, it seemed silly to say the thing that just happened to you never should have happened, but he said it anyway.

Once we were back on the road, Mr. Westgard

NOT MAKING GOOD SPEED ON THE WAY TO THE SANTA FE TRAIL.

picked up his conversation from three days earlier as though it had ended only a minute ago.

"So after I had worked for the Century Map Company for a number of years, pushing my trundle wheel across these glorious states of ours, I had the opportunity one day to be speaking with the commander of Fort Apache, Arizona, where we will be making camp during this very journey.

"And, as I was speaking to the commander of Fort Apache, he told me how the United States Army was about to undertake a survey of the Santa Fe Trail to see if it might prove practical for the use of motorized vehicles.

"Naturally, upon hearing this—and being a mapmaker of some repute—I offered up my services to the federal government of these glorious states of ours."

This offer was accepted, and Mr. West-gard worked with the American army for a number of years after, mapping routes that the new horseless carriages and military convoys might one day take through the western states and territories leading into California, Oregon, and Washington.

There weren't many cars or trucks around to actually test these routes. Mr. Westgard didn't even own a car back then. This was well before Henry Ford brought out the Model T, and most cars in the United States were expensive as all get out—even those tin-cup contraptions carriage makers in New York City sold at the turn of the century. Why, they had had no brakes or a reverse gear, just an engine that turned the wheels.

All Mr. Westgard owned in those days was a Schwinn bicycle, which he rode everywhere, the trundle wheel strapped to a cart he pulled behind him. The army had to loan him some of its motorized vehicles to test his routes: some Wintons and Fords, a Republic truck once. He told us that getting behind the wheel of those vehicles was like falling in love, which didn't surprise me all that much. If the man loved pushing a wheel across the United States, why wouldn't he love strapping a motor to one and riding on top?

He saved his money from the army and bought his first automobile in 1907. After that, you couldn't keep Mr. Westgard in one place too long. Where he could go now that he owned a horseless carriage, well, it wasn't endless. But it was close enough to endless to drive right up to her and give her a kiss.

Howie Starts an Argument

That night we camped in Husted, which was little more than a railway siding for the Denver and Rio Grande Western Railroad. Mr. Westgard said that, two years earlier, there had been a terrific train crash not far from where we camped when a northbound Denver and Rio Grande train ran head-on into a southbound one.

Ten people had been killed and scores injured. Mr. Westgard had driven through a few days later. The mangled engines of the two trains were still there as were some of the bodies, waiting for an over-worked undertaker to arrive from Colorado Springs.

"It was a ghastly sight," he said. "One of the worst I have seen in this part of the country, and keep in mind, I have seen the bodies of lynched men."

We camped out that night even though there was a roundhouse near us as well as a bunkhouse and a schoolhouse with a painted fence around it. You didn't see much of such a thing as a fence in those parts on account of the wind and the sand. Howie asked why we couldn't sleep in the bunkhouse, and Mr. Westgard replied that he had never had a good night's sleep in a railway bunkhouse and didn't even bother attempting such things anymore.

It was another clear night. While Howie tried to make a fire, Mr. Thompson came over and helped me again with getting the gear out of the truck and starting the supper.

"You don't have to do that," I said to him as he took out the skillets and the tin plates.

"I don't mind, George. Back in Chicago, I often helped out around the house. It would drive my father crazy—he said we had servants for work like that—but building a stable or helping the cooks with a meal, I'd rather do that than push paper around a desk all day."

"So this was your idea to come on the truck run?"

"No, that was Father's. I'm not in school this semester. I'm afraid my grades weren't good enough. Father said I could make myself useful by going on this trip and being his representative.

"So, honestly, I don't mind helping out, George. I guess we can have the canned beef tonight, right?"

A COOK FIRE STARTED AND ENDED MOST DAYS ON THE ROAD.

I hid my surprise at being asked a question by a boss then said the canned beef would work. I would add some bacon and cook some potatoes to go along with it. When the food was cooked, Mr. Thompson and I served it up on the tin plates, along with a pot of strong coffee. Even though it was a clear night, we made sure to pitch a tarp over the firewood. We were all in our bedrolls shortly after supper, and even though I had made that coffee extra strong, it didn't keep any of us awake. I heard Howie snoring before I had bunched up my clothes into a decent-shaped pillow.

The following day, as he was trying to get the morning cook fire going, Howie started to complain.

"That was cold last night," he said. "Why didn't we sleep in the bunkhouse?"

"Have you ever tried to sleep with a roomful of roustabouts?" asked Mr. Westgard.

"No."

"I can assure you, there would have been little sleep for any of us. And if our provisions had remained in the back of the truck during the night, it would have been a miracle akin to our Good Lord walking on water."

Howie didn't say anything for a minute.

"Well, at least we would have been warm," he said finally, poking at some embers in the fire, trying to get the wood to catch. It was such a silly thing to say no one answered him right away. He seemed to take that as a sign he had made a compelling argument and continued: "Yeah, we would have been toasty warm. And roustabouts, I can handle roustabouts easily enough, Mr. Westgard. People in Denver don't give me a hard time. I have some of the best boxing skills in the entire state."

"Just as you are one of the best mechanics?" asked Mr. Thompson. Howie shot him a mean look, which I was pleased to see didn't make Mr. Thompson turn away, and then I guess because Mr. Thompson was paying his salary, Howie didn't say anything else. He just sat around the cook fire sulking, which annoyed all of us although not so much as his talking, so we let it go.

Anyway, if Howie thought he had something to complain about that morning, he was in for a hell of a surprise with the rest of the day.

That day discouraged all of us except Mr. Westgard, who seemed almost cheerful as we made our way toward Colorado Springs.

"This is an adventure, is it not, gentlemen?" he laughed. "Yes, a grand adventure I would say."

The arroyos, which had been challenging enough on the way to Palmer Lake, were now everywhere. Not in a descriptive way, either, the way someone in the bush will tell you the mosquitoes were everywhere, when really they were just around his face. Those ruts in the trail really were everywhere. Not only had the arroyos, dried up gulches, and riverbeds become more plentiful, they had increased in size. I don't even know if arroyos were still the proper words to describe what we had to drive over. They were craters. Upside down hills. For the first time on the trip, we had to stop and use the lumber to build wooden bridges over the gaping holes in the ground.

The land itself had hardened into a hard clay, a land so hard our bones rattled whenever the truck rose and fell through the gulches. To make matters worse, there was now a grade to the road; 20 percent it must have been at times.

Then, in the middle of the afternoon, just to make things interesting, a sand storm hit us, a storm so fierce, it cut my face until it bled. The sand felt like coarse sandpaper ripping across my skin. Even over the howling wind I could hear Howie in the back—our weather expert—complaining that this "shouldn't be happening."

He continued. "How can you have a sand storm right after a snowstorm!" he hollered. "It's not natural. It's those damn witches, I tell you. They must be following us."

I ignored him and kept driving although after half an hour, I had to stop. The road had completely disappeared, and I was worried I would run the truck into one of the arroyos and maybe end our journey. We huddled underneath the canvas tarp strung over the truck bed, having no choice but to wait the storm out.

It didn't stop until midday of the following day. A man could walk from Husted to Colorado Springs in less than a day if the weather held for him. We took two days and still arrived in the middle of the night. There we checked into a hotel, slept on clean sheets, and tried to forget what had just happened to us.

A SANDSTORM ON THE WAY TO NEW MEXICO.

Howie Gets Drunk

The next morning, I checked the truck for damages while Mr. Westgard and Mr. Thompson went to the telegram office to send dispatches. Mr. Westgard sent his telegrams to newspapers and automotive magazines. Mr. Thompson sent his to his father and a list of people his father had given him—my old boss, Mr. Otto; the president of Saurer in New York City; and men who held Saurer distribution rights in California.

Howie stood beside me as I worked on the truck although it soon became apparent there was little damage to anything other than the carburetor, which had to be cleaned of sand and then was right as rain. It also became apparent that Howie didn't know much about trucks or any of the parts that made them run.

"I thought you were the best mechanic in Denver," I said to him in exasperation after he had confused the emergency brake with the air brakes.

"I am a damn fine mechanic," he said angrily. "I just don't know this kind of truck. It's a hell of a lot different from my Black Crow."

A Black Crow. Probably the simplest vehicle on the road if you didn't count cycle-cars. Yes, this would be different.

"Listen," I said. "Why don't you go and get the provisions while I finish up here."

I gave Howie the list of fresh food we wanted to bring with us for the next stage of the trip—eggs, cheese, some more steak—as well as the money Mr. Thompson had given me.

"I saw a grocery on the way into town. A Chinese one, down that street over there," I pointed with my finger at a cross street. "I bet you can get everything there."

Howie took the money and nodded. "Do I spend it all?" he asked.

"Doubt if it will cost that much. No sense getting too much fresh food, or it will rot on us. Just get enough for a few days until we reach Trinidad."

I stuck my head back under the hood of the truck, and Howie walked away. I put oil in the shock pans, drained the radiator, put in fresh water, checked the crate of spare parts (it occurred to me Howie had been the only one to check it. I was glad to see ball bearings), then went back to the hotel to freshen up in my room. I decided to have a nap after that, and it was late afternoon when I awoke.

I went down to the restaurant in the hotel and found Mr. Westgard and Mr. Thompson sitting at a table, reading some old newspapers from Denver.

"Ah, George," said Mr. Thompson when he saw me. "How did the Pioneer Freighter make out these past few days? My father is anxious to know."

"Quite well," I answered. "There was some sand in the carburetor, but that's about it. It's a tough frame we have on that truck."

Mr. Thompson broke into one of his shy smiles, happy to hear what I had just reported.

"My father will be pleased to hear that. And Howie, he agrees?"

I didn't answer right away because Howie was a working man just like me, and no working man wants to speak badly about another working man in front of the boss, even a boss who calls you by your first name and says it's all right for you to do the same thing.

"He certainly does, Mr. Thompson. He didn't find anything wrong at all."

"Well, that is wonderful news. I shall send Father a telegram before we leave tomorrow. By the way, where is Howie?"

Again, I hesitated before answering. He wasn't back yet? Getting the provisions shouldn't have taken him more than an hour.

"I'm not exactly sure. I think he had some errands to run."

Just then, Howie walked into the restaurant. He had packages in his hand—something wrapped in butcher's oilskin paper, a wooden egg crate, a sack of potatoes—and as he walked between the tables, he lurched from side to side, bumping into some diners sitting at one of the tables, knocking a cutlery setting off another.

When he got to our table, he carefully lowered the wooden egg crate to the floor then, in exaggerated hand motions, placed the oilskin parcel on top of the crate and tried to place the sack of potatoes on top of that although he then thought better of it and placed it beside the crate. Finally, he stood up to look at what he had created, frowned, and moved the oilskin parcel off the egg crate as well.

"Gentlemen," he said when he had finished doing all this. "I have brought our provisions."

He took off his cloth cap when he announced this, made a wide sweeping gesture with his hands—a deep bow it was, although his balance was off—and as we were staring at him, he fell face first into the egg crate.

Both Mr. Westgard and Mr. Thompson jumped from their chairs when this happened, Mr. Westgard yelling "My Lord, the man is drunk!" but Howie paid them no mind, just broke into a low, sputtering laugh as he tried to pull his head off the egg crate. His body made a sort of push-up gesture when he did this; he actually had to push three times before breaking free. After dusting himself off, he strode to Mr. Thompson and Mr. West-gard's table and sat down.

"By the way," he said, snapping his fingers at a waiter and looking at Mr. Thompson, "you have just paid me part of my wages."

I guess we had all been drunk before so no one climbed up on Howie's back. On river runs back home, it was almost expected that you would get drunk sometime during the trip; when you moored at Quyon, or Ottawa, or someplace else down river. It was part of the job. Part of the working week. I remember picking up my dad after one of those runs, and he was so drunk he insisted on riding the horse even though I had brought a wagon.

That none of the eggs had broken also helped Howie skate free of the affair. When he stumbled off to bed, Mr. Westgard went so far as to hold the crate in his arms and marvel at the workmanship that had gone into a simple egg crate.

"Look at this," he said, pointing to the place where Howie's head had left a deep indent. "They have reinforced the lid with transverse slats." Mr. Thompson looked to where he was pointing and agreed it was remarkably thorough workmanship. When they were finished the egg crate inspection, I offered to take the provisions up to my room for the night, saying I would load them into the truck first thing in the morning.

"That's a capital idea, Mr. MacLean," said Mr. Westgard. "I suspect Mr. Grey might not be up to the task."

I didn't bother saying I had yet to see the task Howie *would* be up for. Instead, I put the parcels under my arms and made my way to my room. As I left, I heard Mr. Thompson say maybe this was not a bad thing what had happened. He doubted if Mr. Grey would feel much like talking or complaining when we left the next day.

We left Colorado Springs on March 9, and the next week was one of the longest of my life. I know it sounds funny to say that because a week is always a week, time never changes, but try and tell that to your body — or your head, for that matter. The arroyos between Colorado Springs and Trinidad were from another time and place. Nothing natural. Nothing I had seen before. It was like the earth had been blown up; as if a battalion of cannons had let loose a barrage on the road in front of us.

We were constantly hauling lumber from the back of the truck to build bridges or to replace wooden culverts. I don't know if there was a single arroyo on this stretch of road that we managed to cross without the aid of wood.

Within a few days of this routine, we became quite proficient at "jumping" the truck over culverts and gulches. The method

A FEW OF THE ROAD CONDITIONS FACED BY THE PIONEER FREIGHTER.

of crossing them consisted of pushing a plank under one of the rear wheels, wrapping one end of a chain around the tire and the other around the forward end of the plank, and then throwing the truck into first gear and running the engine as fast as I could while "jumping in" the clutch.

The truck literally flew over the holes whenever we did this. The plan had been Mr. Westgard's idea, and it was a wonder how well it worked. It was even more of a wonder we didn't strip the gears or completely mangle the clutch. The more I drove the Pioneer Freighter, the more impressed I became with the truck. If we had pulled such a stunt in Howie's Black Crow, the car would have been junk by the end of the day.

The storms kept coming, too. When we approached Walsenburg, we hit another sand storm, this one just as strong and vicious as the one outside Husted. Knowing what was coming, we didn't even try to drive through it: we just put the truck into park and crawled underneath the covered bed to wait it out.

Then, just south of Walsenburg, we hit a snowstorm. Howie, by this time, was beside himself, saying for most of the day: "How can you have a snowstorm the day after a sand storm? It's not natural. I tell you, it's witch-craft. Those witches want us to turn back."

Walsenburg, I found out later, was the hometown of Robert Ford, the man who shot Jesse James. After ten days on the road, we were all feeling a bit like Robert Ford. And Howie was looking an awful lot like Jesse James.

Funny thing was, as soon as the snow stopped falling, the sun came up, the sky cleared almost instantly, and I found myself looking at two huge mountains that seemed to have sprung up during the storm. They were snow-capped and mammoth, and looked downright imperial sitting there without a mountain range near them vying for your attention. The Spanish Peaks, Mr. Westgard called them and explained that they were an important landmark on the Santa Fe Trail; one that could be seen as far away as Colorado Springs.

I looked at them in wonder. Found myself in no great hurry to leave. But we kept going and finally reached Trinidad on March 15. We had been on the road for eleven days and had travelled just under 200 miles.

Getting Rid of Howie

The morning after we reached Trinidad, I got a knock on my hotel-room door. When I opened the door, Mr. Thompson was standing there, his wide-brimmed hat in his hand, his feet shuffling nervously on the thin carpet of the hallway.

"George, do you mind if I come in?"

I told him I didn't mind, and he walked nervously into my room, looking around at the unmade bed and the clothes I had pulled from my satchel the night before, most of which had been left on the floor.

"I need your advice," he said. "It is rather a delicate matter, and as it will affect you, I wanted to talk to you first."

A boss who wanted my advice? I was starting to like Mr. Thompson, appreciated the work he did on the road and around the campfire. He was a good kid. But he was making me uncomfortable. It wasn't natural for a boss to want my advice. Or to give a whit about my feelings. I would have to explain that to him one day. Pull him aside and explain he really was the boss, and he needed to start acting like one. But instead of saying any of this, I said:

"What is it you want to talk to me about, Mr. Thompson?"

"Please . . . Arthur. Well, I have been keeping my father apprised of our trip—what each of us is mostly responsible for and our progress and the like. I send and receive telegrams at every town we reach. He has been asking me many questions about Howie. I have answered him truthfully."

I told him I knew about the telegrams.

"Well, there was a telegram waiting for me when we arrived in Trinidad last night. It seems my father wants me to . . . he wants me to . . . well, he wants me to fire Howie."

So there it was, and I felt even more uncomfortable than I had when I opened the door: my boss was now telling me about firing someone before he actually got around to doing the firing. Which was why I needed to talk to Mr. Thompson one day soon. I didn't need to know this. Nor was I all that happy knowing it.

I guess it's the way I was brought up or maybe the place I was brought up, for there were certainly some bad lumbermen around

Campbell's Bay. There were probably bad lumbermen everywhere, the kind of men you never wanted to be stuck on a timber crib with, but I never liked seeing a man get fired for it. It seemed like that was what made bosses different from everyone else. The fact they could fire you and throw your whole life upside down. Unless a guy was trying to kill you, I always figured there had to be a better way.

"My father says I should do it right away," Mr. Thompson continued, "but I wanted to check with you first, George. Can we get by with just the three of us?"

I said we probably could.

"I thought so as well. My father says Howie has not been truthful with us, is lazy, probably a drunkard, and these are all firing offenses. That's what he calls them. Firing offenses."

I didn't say anything. Just looked at Mr. Thompson and said nothing.

"How would you feel about this, George?"

"I don't like seeing any man get fired."

"I thought you might say that."

We stared at each other for a few seconds, both of us uncomfortable, me wishing the firing had happened without me knowing about it beforehand. I wasn't expecting Mr. Thompson to change his mind, especially if his father had told him to fire Howie, so what had either of us gained by him knocking on my hotel-room door?

"Well, let me talk to Mr. Westgard and see what we can do. You have done a wonderful job for us, George. It would be a shame to put you in a bad mood."

When Mr. Thompson left, I wasn't sure anymore if Howie would be fired. Maybe he was about to get a stern warning or something like that. But it was early in the trip, and I had no idea how clever Mr. Westgard could be at times.

That night, after Howie had stumbled back from his errands, we all went for a wonderful supper in the restaurant of the Columbia Hotel. We dined on braised lamb and fresh green beans; even had three bottles of wine between us. Near the end of the supper, Mr. Thompson patted his lips with a napkin, pushed his chair back from the table, and with great ceremony, took a billfold from his inside coat pocket.

"Howie," he said when the billfold was on the table, "you have done wonderful work these past ten days. I know I said I would pay your first wages when we reached Santa Fe, but given your performance, I thought I would pay you now."

He took some bills from the billfold and slid them across the table. Howie counted them, and a fleeting look of surprise crossed his face although he hid it quickly and didn't say anything.

"There is a bonus there as well. You have surely earned it."

Howie broke into a wide grin.

"Thank you, Arthur. I was beginning to think I wasn't appreciated around here."

"Banish the thought, Howie. We all know what sort of man you are."

This brought another smile to Howie's face. He reached across the table and slapped me on the back.

"Old George here isn't bad, either, you know. He can pull his weight most days."

I didn't say anything. Just sat there wondering what in the world was happening. Were we all drunk? Was this some sort of drunken, wide-awake dream I wouldn't remember the next day? Just as I was thinking this, Mr. Westgard said:

"Well, gentlemen, I should retire for the evening. If you were wise, you would all do the same. It's a brave new world in front of us tomorrow."

This didn't register with Howie right away. Either he was too drunk or too happy about the money in his pocket, but Mr. Westgard had to say it again as he pushed his chair away from the table.

"Yes, a brave new world tomorrow."

This time Howie heard him.

"What do you mean, a brave new world?"

"Why, Mr. Grey, the easy part of our journey is behind us. Tomorrow, we shall be entering New Mexico. The real work will begin then."

With that, Mr. Westgard bid us goodnight. Mr. Thompson put away his billfold and did likewise. I sat with Howie for a few minutes, waiting to see if he was going to say anything, but he seemed to be in shock, so I left him sitting there as well.

The next morning when we got no reply to repeated knockings on his door, a front-desk clerk told us Howie Grey had left sometime in the middle of the night.

"He seemed in quite a hurry," said the clerk.

Karl Benz, Gottlieb Daimler, and the Santa Fe Trail

On our way out of Trinidad, Mr. Westgard told us he had gotten rid of many "less than adequate" hired hands with the same trick. Tell them horror stories about what lay down the road—the river that would drown them, the quicksand that would devour them, the mountain that would crush them—and people like Howie Grey disappeared like morning dew.

"Mr. Grey was relatively easy," he said. "He didn't even ask any questions."

If he had, Mr. Westgard would have told him a story that, whittled down, said entering New Mexico was like having the hounds of hell descend upon you.

"Keep in mind," he cautioned, "these stories work because they are entirely true. People like Mr. Grey are such proficient liars they can normally tell when someone is doing the same thing back to them."

Not feeling terribly comforted by this, I continued driving, looking around the countryside and marvelling at how it had changed in the past few days. Gone were the grasslands of the Great Plains. The land was now

a hard, red clay, which almost glowed in the early morning light as far as I could see in any direction. The mountains had inched closer as well, the Raton Pass not that far away according to our map. It was a high cut through the Sangre de Cristo Mountains that would divide the Santa Fe Trail into two directions.

The truck was running well, and with no bad weather and no complaining from Howie, it was altogether a pleasant morning. We reached Starkville, the last settlement we would pass through in Colorado, by midmorning. Starkville was a mining town with shafts dug into the foothills and wooden timbers showing the entranceways to the mines. We observed scores of the little holes as we drove by, so many of them that the hills looked like some termite-eaten hunk of wood.

We could see men coming in and out of the shafts. A small knot of men congregated at the railway siding for the Denver and Rio Grande Western train. There wasn't much more than that to Starkville, and we drove right through without stopping.

Before we were clear of the town, though, another car passed us in the opposite direction, something that surprised me so much, I almost hit the brakes. It was like a boulder rolling our way or something. Turned out to be a Model T that someone had cut the back off of and welded a bed on, so it could carry cargo. In this case, the payload was a load of coal on its way to the railway siding.

"I think that man could use one of your father's fine Saurer trucks," said Mr. Westgard, looking at the car as it passed and giving the driver a small wave of his hand. "It really is quite remarkable where you find cars these days. Not so many years ago, we would have been the only ones on the road."

I didn't bother to mention that the cut-up Model T car was the first motorized vehicle we had seen during our many days on the road, so instead of one horseless carriage in the middle of nowhere, there were now two—which didn't seem like the giant leap forward Mr. Westgard was making it out to be. Still, he talked about the future of horseless carriages morning, noon, and night; how far they had come, how far they would go. Some nights he was talking about them even as I fell asleep, so it was the last thing I heard in the day, the thing I went on to dream about.

One of the first things I read in those Britannicas later on when our trip was long over, and I was back home in Campbell's Bay, was a long story on the history of the automobile. It was funny. Some of the stuff I read made me laugh out loud; so much so, my wife asked what could be so funny in an encyclopedia, and when I told her, she gave me a queer look. What can I say? I'm crazy about trucks and cars.

Who built the world's first car? I guess that depends on whether you count steam engines, which I'm inclined not to, but if you did, then it was a Frenchman named Nicolas-Joseph Cugnot. He designed a steam-powered tractor for the French army in 1769. Built it at the Paris arsenal. According to the Britannicas, the tractor had a top speed of two-and-a-half miles an hour and had to stop every ten minutes to wait for the steam pressure to come back up. It had three wheels.

Somehow, even with a top speed of two-and-a-half miles an hour and rest stops every ten minutes, Cugnot still managed to crash his car into a stone wall just outside Paris. According to the Britannicas, this was the world's first traffic accident.

Anyway, if you're one of those people who believes a car or truck should have an internal combustion engine and run on gasoline or diesel like I do, then the first car was actually invented not that long ago, just like Mr. Westgard kept on telling us around the cook fire. It happened in Germany although people can't agree on which German actually did it.

It might have been a mechanical engineer named Karl Benz, or it might have been a

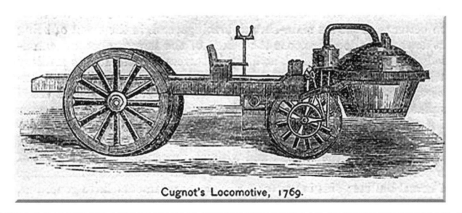

Cugnot's Locomotive, 1769.

THE WORLD'S FIRST AUTOMOBILE, BUILT BY NICOLAS-JOSEPH CUGNOT IN 1769.
Appleton's Journal

THE CAR THAT CHANGED EVERYTHING — HENRY FORD'S MODEL T.
Shipler Commercial Photographers, Harry Shipler, 1910.

fellow named Gottlieb Daimler. People can't agree on who was first because there are arguments to be made for both men. In 1886, the German government gave Benz a patent for a gas-powered vehicle, which was the first patent given for such a thing anywhere in the world. (This patent was also for another three-wheeled vehicle, like they didn't have enough rubber in Europe or something.)

A few years later, Benz came to his senses and designed a four-wheeled vehicle, patenting that vehicle in 1891. By 1900, his company—it didn't have the word Mercedes in it back then—was the largest car company in the world. So it could have been Karl Benz who built the first car. Or it could have been Gottlieb Daimler, who built a gas-powered car in 1885 but didn't get around to patenting it until a few years later.

The Britannicas had diagrams for both cars, and I have to say it was Daimler's that looked most like a car. It had a vertical cylinder. A gasoline injected-carburetor. Four wheels. So I'm partial for Daimler, although to be honest, I might be biased because the encyclopedia also said he invented the first truck. He did that in 1896. Attaching a cargo bed to a metal chassis, he hooked the whole thing up to an internal combustion engine and off he went—truckin'.

People laughed at Daimler when he built a truck because they didn't see the point of the invention. It went slower than a team of horses. Would never be able to compete with a train for the forwarding of goods and cargo. So why bother? God love him, though, because he kept tinkering with the thing: adding new features, increasing the speed, expanding the cargo bed. It was a matter of pride with him proving all the naysayers wrong. I found it real easy to like the guy.

Here in North America, the first people to build a car were some bicycle mechanics from Springfield, Massachusetts, the Duryea brothers—Charles and Frank. They built a gas-powered vehicle in 1893. Now, you would think being first would give you some sort of advantage in this world, some sort of head start on everyone coming up behind you, but I had never heard of the Duryea brothers. When I read a little further, I understood why. Duryea automobiles didn't have brakes. Nor did the brothers see that as a problem that needed to be fixed.

When the brothers took their car around trying to sell it, giving demonstrations in cities up and down the Northeastern Seaboard, they would stop the thing by driving into a curb. What could be easier? Hit something and it stops. "It is not that difficult a maneuver once you have mastered it," Frank Duryea once told a reporter in Philadelphia.

So that car never caught on. Henry Ford's cars did, though. Same with Ransom Olds's cars. And Jonathan Maxwell's. And Alexander Winton's. All those men thought putting brakes in a car was a smarter thing to do than running it into the curb.

I also read that Henry Ford wasn't the man who invented the assembly line although he often gets bragging rights for it. Assembly lines, the story said, could be found in Europe centuries before Henry Ford started making automobiles in Michigan. Ford wasn't even the first American automaker to use an assembly line. That was Ransom Olds, who I already mentioned knew enough to add brakes to his cars. He created an assembly line in 1901 to manufacture the Olds Curved Dash. In just one year of mass production, the Curved Dash went from 425 cars sold annually to more than 2,500.

What Henry Ford did was refine the assembly line—starting with his Model T in 1908—improving on the idea every year until he got it down so pat that, by 1915, he could manufacture a Model T in three minutes, bumper to bumper, even with a coat of paint. The paint job actually became a problem because none of the regular paint would dry quick enough. The only paint that did was a colour called Japan Black, so for the next eleven years, black cars were the only ones Ford made.

People always talk about Henry Ford, and how his assembly line made the automobile affordable for most Americans. I guess that's true; you'd be a damn fool to argue it. What people don't talk about all that much is how it put everyone else out of business. Before the three-minute car, there were hundreds of automobile manufacturers in the United States: Maxwell, Reo, Packard, Winton, Peerless—a lot of the big names probably still ring some bells with people. Or their advertising pitches would (like Packard's "Ask the man who owns one," or the "Peerless Girls," high-class models who actually showed a bit of ankle).

And the car manufacturers were just the tip of the iceberg. Throw into the mix the motorcycle companies (Indian, Harley-Davidson, Metz) and the cycle-car companies (Hawk, American, O-We-Go), and you get an idea just how busy things were back then. America was just jammed up with people tinkering around with gas-powered cars. Then the motorized assembly line came along, and there was only one way to play.

Still, it was a hell of a run while it lasted. The Packard Twin-Six Touring Car, the Peerless 56, the Cadillac Model A. Those were some of the most beautiful cars ever made to my way of thinking.

A Truck Demonstration

Mr. Thompson gave some demonstrations of his own as we made our way across America. His father had given him a satchel full of brochures. You could tell that the kid would have liked nothing more than to make a sale — pull into town one night and telegram his father with news he'd just sold a truck and to ship it tomorrow to Trouble, New Mexico, or Golden Sunset, Arizona.

He normally gave his demonstrations in the evening when we had arrived in a mining camp for the night. The miners were looking for coal or iron ore or gold, and were mostly immigrants from Europe. It was an adventure every time we tried to sell a truck.

"How much dat carry?" they would ask Mr. Thompson when he had started his presentation, my boss proudly answering: "We figure it's carrying around four tons right now."

"Four donnes?"

"Yes, four tons. The truck itself is another four and-a-half tons. All loaded, we're about 17,000 pounds, gentlemen."

Upon hearing this, the miners would murmur among themselves, their voices low and unbelieving, speaking in languages with plenty of harsh consonants and clipped syllables that neither of us understood.

"Teven-teen daw-sand pound?"

"That's right. We started from Denver earlier this month. We're going to carry the load all the way to Los Angeles and then to New York. A Saurer truck, gentlemen. We're going to show you that with a Saurer truck you won't need mules anymore."

Mr. Thompson then went on to extol the advantages of a truck over a mule. He did this by asking the miners where the nearest railway siding was. They would answer something like "teventy miles," or "one dundred miles."

So they needed to transport their coal by wagon and mule. A team of mules, no doubt. Two men would have to go — at least two men — although two would probably do it. It would be, what, a four- or five-day trip?

"Por," the miners would answer, or "pif or "tix."

So a return trip would be between ten days to a fortnight. The provisions and camping equipment for such a trip, how much

THE PIONEER FREIGHTER, PARKED AT A MINING CAMP IN NEW MEXICO.

space would that occupy in your wagon? Mr. Thompson, a sharp kid, usually asked that question really quick, knowing no one was expecting it.

"Vat?" the one miner who usually did most of the talking and translating would ask.

"How much space does your gear occupy? Your tents and food? In the wagon, instead of having coal, how much gear do you put in?"

"Ahh, yeet," and then there would be a debate among the miners until they finally agreed it was one-quarter the space or one-third the space.

"So imagine, gentlemen, getting a load of coal, a COMPLETE load of coal, to the railway siding and back in TWO days!"

There would be a frantic murmur in the crowd after that, some people thinking they understood what Mr. Thompson had just said but wanting to verify with the translator; others, not understanding any English at all but hearing the shouted questions from their friends now asking, in disbelief, how such a thing could be possible. What sort of lunatic would say such a thing?

"Dis ding," the translator would say, "it go dat past?"

"Yes."

More murmuring in the crowd. People coming up to touch the truck timidly as though it might be hot. Mr. Thompson would then ask me to start the engine, and I would. Men who were standing by the hood of the truck were often startled when it roared to life; they were waiting for me to come out to the front of the vehicle and turn a crank.

Once the truck was going, we would careen through the mining camp all laid out with its army-issue tents and mechanical sloughs; sitting in the bed of the truck, the miners would hoop and holler and give us directions we couldn't understand. Almost always, they would start drinking, asking us to stop at a still or another miner's tent to grab a bottle. Lubricated by drink, they would begin to sing songs I think were called polkas, passing around a bottle of wheat alcohol and yelling "shnell, shnell," which we gathered to mean "faster, faster."

After we were done driving through the camps, Mr. Thompson would gamely thrust a Saurer sales pamphlet into the hands of whoever was the translator.

"For your consideration," he would say, leaving the sentence unfinished, a high-class way of asking someone if they wanted to buy what you were selling. It was a trick he must have learned from his father although, most times when I saw him do this, the translator shoved the pamphlet into his soot-stained jacket and stumbled back to his tent.

Occasionally, as we looked at the man's back retreating in the night, we would hear something like:

"No mules. Dat crazy guy mutt be drunk."

Or:

"Dat crazy ding make me sick," and the miner would throw up over his boots.

New Mexico

Howie's absence didn't slow us down any. But to be fair to him, getting the camp set up or getting the truck across arroyos was really only a three-man job. Mr. Thompson and Mr. Westgard would brace the wood and hook it up to the chains, I would jump the truck over the gulch, then we'd throw everything in the back of the truck as fast as we could. We tried to complete the task a little more quickly each time, loving the simplicity of it, the joy you find sometimes in physical work.

Over the next few days—though the work was hard and the days were long—we fell into a routine that became quite comfortable and familiar; we even managed to keep up with the fixed schedule Mr. Westgard had marked on his map. Why, we were so busy, we drove through the Raton Pass without knowing we were doing it. The pass was like some fat-lipped grin cut into the mountains—so wide, we didn't know what we had done until we looked around and realized we were surrounded by mountains.

After that, the Great Plains were behind us, and we were in New Mexico good and proper, driving through the Maxwell Land Grant, which was once the largest privately held piece of land in the United States. Mr. Westgard told us how the land was first granted to a French Canadian trapper by a Spanish governor who had been tricked by his secretary—who just happened to be a business partner of the trapper's.

The governor granted the land without ever seeing it. Just signed the deed his secretary gave him. The land had not even been surveyed but was described on the paper the secretary handed to the governor as "the tall butte to the north of the Franciscan mission, running east to the salt creek running out of Camp Trouble, then south . . ." That sort of a deed.

When New Mexico became part of the United States, the land was finally surveyed, and it turned out that the governor had given away 1.7 million acres of land. When gold was discovered on the land, that upset a lot of people, but an American court upheld the grant.

"The legality of the grant was unassailable," said Mr. Westgard. "A deal was a deal. It

**THE SOLID RUBBER GOODRICH TIRES ON THE SAURER TRUCK
NEVER HAD TO BE REPLACED.**

was the governor's fault for not checking more carefully. Caveat emptor and all that."

He paused for a minute and looked around, perhaps trying to imagine what 1.7 million acres of land would look like if you spread it all down in the form of a road.

"It seems," he said finally, "that the governor could have used the services of a good pathfinder."

We were travelling across the Colorado Plateau now, which some people might tell you is still part of the Great Plains even though it's nothing like the plains. We were surrounded by buttes and canyons, all of the land covered with sand even though we were weeks away from the Sonoran Desert. There were suddenly plenty of irrigation ditches as well, most of them with wooden culverts or even bridges. Few of the bridges were strong enough to support the weight of an eight-and-a-half-ton truck, though, so we had to stop, get the lumber from the back of the bed, stretch it out over the ditch, make it wide enough so our four back wheels could get across, then pack everything up again until we reached the next ditch.

**THE PIONEER FREIGHTER WAS THE LARGEST VEHICLE ON THE
ROAD IN 1911, WHICH CAUSED MANY A TIGHT TURN.**

Sometimes the ditches were so close together, it didn't even make sense to jump back into the truck, so Mr. Westgard and Mr. Thompson walked beside the truck with the lumber hanging out back, not a lick of shade anywhere to protect them from the scorching sun. Not every day does the driver have the best job, but I sure did on that stretch.

Over the next few days, we drove and walked our way down the Santa Fe Trail, passing through Maxwell, Springer, and Wagon Mound, which got its name because of a large butte nearby shaped like a Conestoga wagon. We spent our nights in mining camps, Mr. Thompson, trying to sell a truck. Never having much luck.

We were heading in a southwesterly direction, not having yet committed fully to making the hard turn west. That would happen in Albuquerque, after which we would travel pretty much straight west, following the sinking sun all the way to Los Angeles.

There wasn't much in the way of vegetation anymore to speak of, just some sagebrush and the odd patch of stunted ponderosa pine you found near a creek or a stream. With nothing to hold the sand down, it covered everything—our clothes, hair, bedrolls, pots, pans, food. We tried to cover up as best we could, but it was a losing battle. We finally gave up and lived with the discomfort.

When we forded the Gallinas River, we had to use the winch for the first time, hooking the line up to what would have been called a big old Jack Pine, back home, then pulled ourselves across. The water lapped right over the frame of the truck when it hit the middle channel; the wheels weren't even touching, and we were momentarily a boat.

The town we were trying to reach in those days was Las Vegas, a town big enough to have its own electrical streetcar, Carnegie Library, and no less than four high-class hotels. We would be staying at one of them—the Plaza. It was also a railway town: The Atchison, Topeka and Santa Fe Railway reached there in 1880; but that's not the whole truth. The engineers in charge of laying down the track as the rail line was being built decided it was easier and cheaper to run the line one mile east of Las Vegas.

A lot of things in life, you don't see coming. Maybe most things. So no one saw what the final placement of that rail line would do to Las Vegas. The distance was great enough to discourage disembarking passengers from travelling directly to town, and before long, an entirely new town had sprung up

around the railway siding called—and it must have taken some time to come up with the name—East Las Vegas. This new settlement was not incorporated and did not, therefore, fall under the jurisdiction of the sheriff, judge, and mayor of Las Vegas; as a result, it became a sort of no-man's land. Not even the railway company would take responsibility for the town, and almost immediately, East Las Vegas attracted the type of people who liked unincorporated, sheriff-less, no-man lands: Billy the Kid, Jesse James, Doc Holliday and his girlfriend Big Nosed Kate, Wyatt Earp, the Durango Kid—they all spent time there. Even Handsome Harry the Dancehall Rustler called it home for a spell.

"Thank goodness those days are behind us," said Mr. Westgard as we approached Las Vegas, stopping the truck one more time, pulling out our lumber, and laying the boards across the railway tracks. "It would have been a dangerous place not that long ago."

Neither Mr. Thompson nor I said anything as we were too tired for conversation. We still didn't say anything when we passed the dancehalls, hotels, and saloons of East Las Vegas. A half hour later, we were in Las Vegas proper, making our way to the Plaza Hotel by following the electric streetcar line right to the front door. We were going to be in Las Vegas for two nights, getting new provisions, sending telegrams. Mr. Westgard was to speak the following night before a local

FOR MOST DAYS ON THE ROAD, OAK PLANKING WAS USED AS OFTEN AS GASOLINE AND OIL.

Good Roads committee.

There was also a fellow who owned a garage in Las Vegas, who Mr. Thompson needed to meet. His father had left instructions to see the man as his garage was the only one in Las Vegas, and he was thinking about selling horseless carriages to go along with the gasoline and oil he was already selling.

"Ensure he has a Saurer demonstration before leaving Las Vegas," the telegram had said. "He has never heard of a truck. You must convince him of the need."

This would be Mr. Thompson's first demonstration outside of a mining camp, and he seemed nervous about it. He instructed me several times that I would need to be available for the demonstration and that I couldn't disappear like Howie did, running errands. He did this even though he was the boss and only needed to tell me once.

"The man has never heard of a truck, George. In a town this size. Does that surprise you?"

I told him it did to make him feel good and to let him know it wasn't some freakish contraption he was trying to sell the man. But, to be honest, most people back then had never heard of a truck.

Jack Mack and a Hard Sell

It wasn't a great surprise that most people in 1911 had never heard of a truck. There simply weren't that many people making them. There may have been hundreds of automobile companies in the United States back then, but there weren't nearly as many truck companies. Until the Great War, not many people saw the point of owning a truck.

Some of the larger car companies—Ford, Packard, Oldsmobile—had started making trucks by 1911. Even some of the bicycle companies—the ones with a motorized vehicle prototype they couldn't sell—had come up with a cargo-carrying motorized vehicle prototype that they couldn't sell. And some European companies were coming into the market, like Saurer. But an American company making trucks and nothing but trucks, there was really only one to talk about back then, and I've always rather liked Mack Trucks because of that.

I read in the Britannicas that the first Mack truck idea came to Jack Mack in a dream around 1900 after he had spent six years tinkering with steam engines and electric engines in the back of his wagon and carriage shop in Brooklyn, New York. Those early inventions never seemed to work, so he drove most of them off a wharf into the East River.

Jack Mack was a self-trained mechanic just like me; a brawny German kid from Scranton, Pennsylvania, who ran away from the farm at the age of fourteen to become a teamster. In 1890, he was working at a carriage and wagon company in Brooklyn when the owner retired. Mack bought the company and went into partnership with his youngest brother Augustus, who had left the farm, just like Jack, but had gone off to business college.

One of the first things the Mack brothers did, and I laughed when I read this, was get out of the carriage business. They wanted to build wagons, not fancy carriages: cargo-moving, pull-up-to-the-back-of-the-factory, splash-mud-on-your-gators wagons. A workingman's vehicle.

They built a pretty good wagon, too. Developed a niche market for milk wagons until nearly every dairy in New York was using a Mack wagon. The Mack brothers (there were five of them, and they all ended up working at Mack Trucks at one time or another) were doing well in the wagon trade. Then Jack Mack had that dream—a vision he called it later—of a motorized wagon that wasn't built from castaway automobile parts like most trucks were in those days; a truck that was tough and dependable and could give trolley cars, livery teams—hell, maybe even the railways—a run for their money.

So Mack approached a man named Isaac Harris. Harris had just been given a contract to conduct sightseeing tours in Prospect Park in Brooklyn, and Mack convinced him he should use a motorized trolley for his tours; that there was no such thing in the world as a motorized trolley didn't seem to worry Harris for some reason. He gave the Macks money to start the project.

You almost have to wonder about a man's dreams when you hear a story like Jack Mack's because he ended up building exactly what he envisioned even though every other vision had become spawning grounds for fish in the East River. Tough? That first Mack vehicle ferried people around Prospect Park for nearly a quarter century before being shipped off to

JACK MACK—
THE ORIGINAL "BULLDOG."

work someplace else for a few more years. It had well over a million miles on its odometer when it was last seen.

News of the motorized miracle soon spread throughout New York City, and suddenly the Mack brothers had something they never had before—orders from paying customers for a motorized vehicle. Before long, the brothers were filling orders for motorized trolleys—buses people started calling them—from across the United States. They soon needed more factory space and moved to Allentown, Pennsylvania, where one of the Mack brothers had a silk farm.

In 1905, the Macks built their first truck: a five-ton cab-over-the-engine design that also sold well. All of a sudden, Jack Mack had the Midas touch; all his crazy old ideas were now working. By 1911, the company employed 825 people and sold more than 600 trucks and buses a year.

But the brothers (there was Jack, Gus, Charley, Willie, and Joseph) hit a problem that same year. When they started in the truck business, the market was theirs: nothing was out there except the laughter of everyone who thought they were crazy. But when the

Mack brothers showed that there was a market for motorized cargo vehicles, suddenly others wanted in on it. Ford, Peerless, Pierce-Arrow—the big companies wanted to jump into the truck market.

So, in September 1911, Mack Trucks merged with Saurer, a deal put together by New York City financier J.P. Morgan to make sure the two companies would have more money and could better compete against the big boys. Morgan called the new company the International Motor Company (IMC).

The board meetings at IMC must have been something. I've seen photos of J.P. Morgan, and he was one of those fancy robber-baron types—top hat, three-piece suits, and what have you. I can imagine him sitting on one side of the table (maybe next to the men from Switzerland), the Swiss guys looking at production tables and flow charts. On the other side of the table would have been the Mack brothers of Scranton, Pennsylvania.

IMC was a bad marriage that couldn't last. In two years, Jack Mack stormed out of a board meeting, upset with Morgan's plan to sell some of the company's assets to raise money.

"Why sell your own company?" Jack Mack asked him. "What kind of stupid plan is that?"

All the other brothers left soon afterward except for Willie, who stayed until he retired in the late '20s. Morgan was smart enough to keep the Mack name, though; even changed the entire company back to being called Mack

Trucks when the Mack AC came out. The AC was a light-model truck that got heavy praise in the Great War. It even earned the company its nickname, "Bulldog," because that's what Allied troops thought of whenever they saw the grill of the truck rising and falling through the trench line—a sturdy bulldog on its way to save them.

Bulldog became part of the company's lore even though the original bulldog had stormed out of the company five years earlier, saying he was going to show Morgan how to run a truck company.

It wasn't hard to find the man who owned the garage. We were, after all, buying gasoline and oil from him.

"So this is a truck," he said, when we parked the Pioneer Freighter in his garage.

"Yes, Mr. Davis, a Saurer four-and-a-half-ton," said Mr. Thompson. "It's called the Pioneer Freighter. We have chosen the name because of its ability to carry freight and also because . . ."

"It's a pioneer. I get it, son," said Mr. Davis, cutting off Mr. Thompson and waving his hand at the same time. "Your father has been in touch with me. I told him I didn't see the point in selling motorized cargo vehicles. Cars, maybe. But not this thing."

"And why is that, sir?"

"Well, we got a train that comes through town. Maybe you seen it?"

THE MACK AC TRUCK

"Yes, sir, we have, but the Pioneer Freighter . . ."

"Train does a fine job moving stuff around for people. Who in the world would ever buy your contraption?"

"Well, sir, that is an excellent question. The potential market for the Saurer Pioneer Freighter would consist of the following groups—miners, particularly those working in . . ."

"Why all the wood?"

"Pardon?"

"Why are you carrying so much lumber, son?"

"Well, the lumber is used to shore up the culverts and bridges we encounter along the way. Also to lay down a corduroy road whenever we . . ."

"Am I supposed to be selling lumber now, too?"

"I'm sorry, Mr. Davis, I don't think I . . ."

"Son, this thing don't make any sense. I told your father that. Sorry he wasted your time by making you come here. Now, do you boys need any gas?"

Mr. Thompson looked as down as a man could be when we left Las Vegas, and nothing either

Mr. Westgard or I said could cheer him up any. He seemed almost shocked that the man at the garage didn't want to go for a demonstration run. Kept apologizing to me for wasting my time. That night, I made a promise to myself: I couldn't put it off one more day. I was going to have to pull him aside and tell him to stop. It made me uncomfortable when he did stuff like apologize to me. Made me not know what to say around him or how to behave.

In the next couple of days, we passed through more mining camps, where Mr. Thompson gave more demonstrations although his heart didn't seem in it. He even forgot to give away his brochures at one camp, and when I pointed this out to him he said:

"I don't think it matters, George. Maybe Mr. Davis was right. What am I supposed to do? Sell every truck with a load of wood so you can get it down the road?"

This upset Mr. Westgard greatly. He actually started to admonish Mr. Thompson.

"The problem is not your fine vehicle, Mr. Thompson," he said. "The problem is these deplorable roads we are forced to drive upon. Give the Good Roads Movement a bit more time, and you will see. There will come a day when people are banging on your doors to buy a motorized cargo vehicle."

This didn't seem to cheer up Mr. Thompson much—maybe he was too young to think about things happening years down the road, or maybe, coming from a rich family and all, he had never been treated as rudely as Mr. Davis treated him. Whatever the reason, we decided to leave him alone as we made our way down the Santa Fe Trail, passing Indian mounds and adobe homes. We had the only truck on the road.

"How Much?"

Three days out of Las Vegas, no mining camp in sight, we parked the truck beside a small creek and pitched our tent for the night. I had just started cooking supper when two Indians arrived on horseback.

They seemed surprised to see a truck in the middle of this clay desert, but were perhaps even more curious about our sign. As they began to ask questions about it, pointing with their fingers, Mr. Westgard tried to explain with his few words of Navaho and a lot of hand gestures that we were travelling a great distance.

"Oooocean . . . to . . . Ooooocean," he said, dragging out the words the way people will talk real slow sometimes, in the hopes that it will somehow make the words easier to understand. It turned out the Indians understood a few words of English, and when Mr. Westgard used the words "big lake" instead of "ocean," they nodded their heads vigorously.

They dismounted after that and walked around the truck. One of them stabbed the coast-to-coast sign with his finger while the other peered inside the canvas-covered bed. The Indian with his head under the tarps called his friend over, and together they stared at our gear for a long time.

Mr. Westgard invited them to share supper with us, and they said: "Yes, yes," laughed, and slapped him on the back a few times as if he were a dear friend who had just re-entered their lives. I cooked beef stew and served it up with cornmeal biscuits and thick slabs of butter. As I was getting the supper ready, Mr. Westgard got his camera from the cab of the truck. Mr. Westgard took a lot of photographs during our trip and fancied himself a bit of a professional. His specialty was landscapes. He didn't like taking photographs of people all that much although whenever we met Indians, he hauled out his camera. The Apaches and Cheyennes didn't care for the sight of Mr. Westgard's camera and would always refuse to pose. The Navahos and Pueblos never seemed to mind.

These two visitors were dressed in a weird mix of clothing. They both had men's dinner vests from a good haberdashery back east, it appeared: leather britches, moccasins, and turquoise jewellery around their wrists and necks. On the head of one of the men was a bowler hat.

THE INTREPID TRAVELLERS, PARKED IN FRONT OF A CHURCH ALONG THE SANTA FE TRAIL.

Mr. Westgard positioned them in front of the Ocean-to-Ocean sign and took several photographs. Then he asked them to move in front of the creek, where he took photos of them sitting on their horses then squatting on the ground. The Indians moved into the various poses without complaint as though they were working for their supper.

"Here good?" one would ask and Mr. Westgard would answer them slowly: "theeeeeere . . . gooooooood."

When he was done, we had supper. Our guests ate quickly without talking to us, just moving their hands from their plates to their mouths and nodding whenever I brandished the stew pot in front of them. Afterward they took corncob pipes from their vest pockets, stuffed the bowls with tobacco, and lit them.

"What call?" asked one of the men, point-ing to the Pioneer Freighter. It was Mr. Thompson who answered.

"It's called a truck."

"Truck?"

"That's right, a truck. It is a motorized cargo vehicle. Like a train, except you own it." Mr. Thompson got one of his brochures. Gave it to the Indians so they could look at the pho-tographs.

The men talked for a minute, pointing at the truck, pointing at the brochure, the tone of their conversation getting more excited. The Indian who had first stuck his head under the tarps went back to the truck and peered again, keeping his head under the tarps for a good five minutes.

When he came back he said to Mr. Thomp-son:

"How much?"

"How cam'st thou in this pickle?"

The next morning, Mr. Thompson was his old self again. Even apologized to us for being "a little blue" as he put it. Mr. Westgard said it was not worth an apology; that anyone who had been in the Good Roads Movement for any length of time—anyone such as himself—knew exactly how he had been feeling.

For the rest of that day, we made our way toward Santa Fe. At times we followed wooden signs fashioned into arrows that pointed the way and said Santa Fe Trail; and as we crashed through a bridge over the Tecolote Creek and passed adobe churches that started to look the same with their red clay vestibules and rectangular-shaped spires, Mr. Westgard gave us a quick lesson on the Good Roads Movement.

Mr. Westgard was a religious man as I might have mentioned already. He carried in his satchel a well-worn Bible and a string of rosary beads. He once told me a Bible translated into Hopi, given to him by a padre at a mission near Phoenix, was one of his most prized possessions. But if you want to know the truth, I think the man had two religions:

One was the Christian faith; the other was the Good Roads Movement.

"Good roads!" he would scream at Mr. Thompson and me almost every day. "Imagine, gentlemen, where we would be right now if the call for good roads had been heard in this far flung county instead of having fallen upon the deaf ears it so obviously has."

He would say stuff like that when we had fallen through a wooden culvert or were up to our axles in mud: "Good roads, gentlemen, imagine it," and Mr. Thompson and I would run around trying to imagine it although we hadn't seen a good road since Denver, so it was a hard thing to imagine.

Mr. Westgard could quote entire passages from *The Gospel of Good Roads*, a pamphlet that was printed five million times before the turn of the century. The cover showed some farmers stranded in a mud sinkhole, one farmer trying to whip a team of horses out of the ruts, the other in the process of abandoning his cart. A caption above the farmers' heads read: "How cam'st thou in this pickle?"

Mr. Westgard used that line all the time.

"Mr. MacLean, Mr. Thompson: how cam'st thou in this pickle?" and we'd be looking at another busted culvert. Or another sink hole. Or another sand storm moving in on us. Point is, he knew that pamphlet backwards and forwards. Said he was even at the convention of the nation's Good Roads committees and Wheelmen's associations held in Providence, Rhode Island, in 1891, when the pamphlet was printed for the first time.

"I was a member of the movement long before I purchased my first automobile," Mr. Westgard told us. "I was an avid cyclist for quite some time. Good Roads. I have been a convert for twenty years."

Rural communities in the United States loved Good Roads people like Mr. Westgard because, when you stopped to think about it, they were right. If you were a farmer in the United States, you spent half your days stuck in mud. Spent the rest of your days fixing the broken axles and split wheels you got from being stuck in mud.

City folks, in particular the fashionable young bicyclists who seemed to be everywhere in those days, also loved Good Roads people. It was cyclists who even started the movement when some bicycle clubs came together in 1890 to form the League of American Wheelmen. Three years later, the league started publishing *Good Roads Magazine*, which, in less than a year, had a circulation of more than a million people.

Even the railway companies liked Good Roads people, which wouldn't strike you right away as likely. The railway companies liked the Good Roads people because, through their efforts, roads would get built to the railway stations and sidings; that meant more farmers would be coming to see them to ship their cattle and produce, and more people would be travelling down the new roads to purchase passenger tickets on their trains.

Many railway companies even funded the cost of building the new roads. It never occurred to any of them—they never caught a glimpse of it from way up there on Mount Railway Olympus—that this might mean competition one day. The railway companies were about as arrogant as it gets back then, and if anyone had mentioned the possibility of competition, the men who owned the railway companies would likely have sneered. A truck? What in the world can such a thing do to hurt us? We own railways.

So they paid for the roads. Or talked their friends in state and territorial governments to have convicts build the roads for them. So prisoners in state and territorial jails were soon dispatched across the country to build macadamized roads, macadamized roads being like the holy grail of the Good Roads Movement. These were roads invented by a Scotsman, John McAdams, who discovered that if you layered three sizes of stone from largest to smallest, they would create a

GEORGE MACLEAN AND ARTHUR THOMPSON PONDER THE LATEST ROAD OBSTACLE.

hard-packed surface when pressure was applied from above. The pressure could come from a steamroller. Or it could come from people simply using the roadway.

A road that got better the more you used it. For Good Roads people, this was more than a revelation. It was a miracle.

Mr. Westgard was even telling us how a macadamized road worked when we saw our first chain gang. It was just before we passed over the Pecos River, and Mr. Westgard figured the convicts must have been shipped by railcar from the territorial prison in Yuma and were likely billeted someplace nearby.

People started calling the road crews chain gangs because the convicts always had their ankles chained together; there was so much metal on the men, it was the glint of steel we saw first when we approached them that first time. As we got nearer, we could see that they were young men for the most part, dressed in black and white pyjamas with bold horizontal stripes separating the colours. They were working with picks and shovels. Some of the men chipped away at the stone outcrops that lined the route; the other men shovelled the stone into a two-foot-deep trench. There must have been close to a hundred men working on the road with about a dozen guards keeping watch. The guards all looked bored and maybe a bit resentful about being outside on such a hot morning. They carried their rifles carelessly in the crook of their arms or leaning against their legs. None of them waved at us as we approached.

You could see that the convicts were breaking rocks into three different sizes, getting ready to lay down a road. There were wagons where they piled the rocks and mules that hauled the wagons to the trench. Looking at the men working with their picks, I was reminded of a photograph I had seen once of a Texas oil field, the rigs all pumping away at the same time, the arc of the rigs looking for all the world like a man's arm thrust overhead as it held a pick.

The sight of the chain gang made us stop talking. Mr. Thompson even averted his eyes. We would see plenty of chain gangs in the next month, and he would eventually stop looking away. That first one, though, was the largest one we would see.

I bumped the truck off the road to give the chain gang plenty of room then drove slowly past, tipping my cap to no one in particular, and maybe that was why no one bothered to wave back. One of the guards even yawned and turned his back to us.

When we had rounded a small mesa and left the chain gang behind, Mr. Westgard continued with his history lesson on the Good Roads Movement. It was as though the chain gang had never existed, as though we had never seen men chained together like livestock, and he had said his last words only a second before.

"The Good Roads Movement was quite a different entity when I first joined, when the temperance clubs were involved, and the Daughters of the American Revolution.

"For many of those people, the movement was about much more than good roads. They were the ones who objected most vigorously to allowing the horseless carriage people onto the various committees. Could not understand what we were doing.

"I fear the movement was a religion to these people instead of good public policy."

I had to smile at that one. Still, I knew what he meant. A lot of the early Good Roads people thought the car and the truck were abominations. They didn't want good roads for just anyone's use. They wanted good roads for bicyclists. The people behind the Great Bicycle Protest in San Francisco in 1896 when tens of thousands of cyclists shut down the city for a day—those people weren't interested in sharing the road with automobiles. Most of them thought cars were the expensive toys of rich people and hated them for it. They were known to put up barbed wire around a parked car.

There was an evangelical, darn near puritan feel to the movement in those days. Bicycling was part of a healthy life, a clean-body, clear-headed sort of thing. It was why the temperance ladies got so heavily involved. Why people like Dr. Kellogg—who ran a sanitarium in upper New York State called Wellville where people did daily breathing exercises and took yogourt enemas—were such cycling enthusiasts.

Anyway, the Good Roads Movement was huge back then even if people tend to forget that today. It had the health people, the bicyclists, the farmers, and the railway men; even became a political party for a while when a Michigan man named Horatio Earle got himself elected to the Michigan state senate as a member of the League of American Wheelmen.

So things were going along pretty well for the Good Roads Movement. Every state and territory had some sort of Good Roads committee or association. Every Daughter of the American Revolution seemed to be a member. Then along came the horseless carriage, and it ruined a perfectly good movement. Changed everything. Suddenly, people like Carl Fisher, Ransom Olds, and Jack Mack were getting themselves elected to the various committees, to the governing boards of the various clubs. Change was rather inevitable after that.

Jack Mack was a man you could imagine doing many things. Having a yogourt enema would not be one of them.

The Childless Widow of Salt Springs

We made our way through San Jose, Ilfeld, Rowe, the southwesterly direction we were travelling in nudging us closer and closer to the mountains. At night, we stayed in mining camps or pitched our tents near a creek or a river where we would often find a stand of ponderosa pine. Under the pine, and with a river running beside us, it was easy to forget we were travelling over the Colorado Plateau. Easy to think I was back home.

We drove by Pueblo ruins just about every day—centuries-old adobe buildings and market stalls being excavated by men wearing starched white shirts, ties, and large-rimmed hats. University people from back east. Wearing the same clothes Mr. Thompson wore every day. One night, we stayed at one of the excavation camps where the men asked a great many questions about the truck. You could see Mr. Thompson getting excited.

"It would be the perfect vehicle for your sort of work, professor," he said, thrusting a pamphlet into the hands of a white-shirted man who looked about as old as the ruins he was excavating. "No need for a mule train after this."

The archeologists were respectful and sober, but the pamphlets still ended up being shoved in their jacket pockets where I'm guessing they were forgotten the next day. You could see Mr. Thompson was disappointed but he didn't get as low as he did in Las Vegas. He told me the next day that university professors would make lousy customers anyway. All they were likely to do after purchasing a truck was complain about something.

"I have spent my entire life around teachers and professors," he said, "and I doubt if any of them could make a trip like ours without complaining about it or writing a book later that made it seem like they had just driven across the country with Homer."

I laughed when he said this. I really was starting to like the kid.

Two days outside of Santa Fe, we got caught in a bad rainstorm, which turned the trail slick and dangerous, and we started to look for a place to stop for the night.

We found a large Mexican adobe, only one storey high although it was a large structure that stretched into the shadows. The men liv-

ADOBE HOMES COULD BE PALATIAL OR RUN-DOWN RELICS LIKE THE ONES ABOVE.

ing in the adobe were shepherds who raised Angora sheep in the foothills. A childless widow offered us her two-room apartment for the night.

The adobe was built near a salt spring on land no one else wanted. There were six families living in the adobe, and their families had been there for many generations. After we arrived, the women cooked bean stew as the men asked questions about the truck. That night, after everyone was fed and asleep, I ventured down the hallway running through the middle of the adobe. I saw that every room branching off the hallway was the same—two

clay rooms with a low-hanging ceiling, straw mats spread on every inch of floor space, children sleeping on top of the mats. At the end of the hallway, I discovered animals. I counted nine pigs and eight dogs, five cats and three burrows, sixteen chickens and an Angora ewe with seven kids.

The next morning, the Mexicans again made us a meal, the childless widow doing much of the work. We were served beans and ground meat cooked in a flour shell. There was fresh coffee as well, and I wondered at their hospitality—at how much meat we were consuming and how little they would have left.

The rain never let up that day, so we stayed another night. We helped out with chores while we stayed inside: fed the animals, chased young boys away from the kitchen, helped make coffee. Mr. Westgard said later that there were some adobes we would see in Santa Fe that had more than 700 rooms.

"Bigger than a modern apartment building in New York City," he stated. I tried to imagine it but couldn't. That would mean thousands of people living in one building. Sharing the same walls. Using the same entranceways.

In a country this big, why would you do it? Just driving through the United States, the way we were doing now, it made me want to see more of it; maybe go north next, find a forest to hunt in where no one would ever find me or pull into a strange town on a Saturday night—East Las Vegas maybe—then hoot and holler and wake up in a bed I'd never slept in before. This country was so crazy big I couldn't get enough of it. Couldn't understand why someone would ever want to settle down, let alone in a single building with thousands of other people.

That night, we were well rested and went to bed long after the sun had set. The childless widow stayed with us as she had no children to watch or man to tend. She told us in broken English that her husband had disappeared one night in a bad storm much like the one we were waiting out. He had made it home but decided to go back out in search of an Angora ram. She wished that she had done more to make him stay.

They had been married three years and had not produced a child. No other man seemed interested in her. It was kind of the people in the adobe to allow her to live in their home, a single woman with her own apartment. Her husband's death had been recent.

We stayed near the salt spring for two days. Waiting out the storm.

A Priest and the Good Roads Movement

Just before we reached Santa Fe, we came to the San Miguel Mission, where you will find the oldest church in the United States, built sometime before 1626. Even though parts of it had been destroyed over the centuries in the various revolts and wars that always seemed to be happening around that part of the country, some of the adobe walls were original.

When we arrived at the church, a priest came out and greeted Mr. Westgard warmly.

"Anton," said the portly, grey-haired man dressed in a white cossack that ran to the balls of his feet, "you have returned."

This was the first time I had heard Mr. Westgard's given name, and I gave a quick double take, wondering if I had heard it correctly. I had never known a man named Anton.

"It is hard to stay away, Father."

"What are you driving this time, Anton?" —yes, Anton—"Have you left room on the road for the rest of us?"

The priest came up to the truck and looked at it in amusement. I took off my cap and climbed out of the Pioneer Freighter, Mr.

Thompson doing the same. When we were standing on the ground, the priest shook our hands warmly.

"It is a truck, Father," said Mr. Westgard once our introductions were finished. "A motorized form of cargo transport. Mr. Thompson, here, his father sells them."

"And what are you transporting, Anton? The tonnage, if you would."

"I figure about four tons. The truck is another four and a half."

"Eight-and-a-half-tons altogether," said the priest. "My dear man, you are a railway engine that has jumped the tracks. However did you get this far?"

And Mr. Westgard told him. Leaving from Denver at the start of the month, the bad snowstorm at Palmer Lake, the sand storms and rain storms after that. Jumping the truck across every irrigation ditch, arroyo, and dry gulch in the territory.

"We're not done, either, Father. We're going to take the truck right down the Trail."

"Down the Trail? With those treads?" And here the priest kicked the rear tires. Not a

A QUICK LUNCH IN FRONT OF AN ADOBE HOME.

gentle kick but a full-blown whomp. "You can't be serious."

Mr. Westgard gave one of those dramatic pauses he liked to use from time to time, left the priest's question hanging, then answered:

"I suppose then, Father, you would have difficulty believing that once we reach the end of the trail we shall promptly turn around and make our way to New York City."

"New York City!" the priest gasped. "Anton, I did not know you were a blasphemer. For how long have you claimed the ability to perform miracles?"

The two men stared at each other. Jaws thrust defiantly outward. Eyes unblinking. And then when I was beginning to wonder what had happened—they seemed friendly enough just a moment before—they burst into laughter.

"May I take her for a drive, Anton?" asked the priest. "I have never before driven eight-and-a-half tons."

"Let's go right now, Father. Are these damnable roads any better?"

"Ahh," said the priest as he held out his hands in an upturned, helpless gesture, "we pray."

The priest, I found out during our drive

around the San Miguel Mission, sat on the board of the Santa Fe County Good Roads Committee. For many years, he had spent most of the money raised in the donation box and on the Sunday morning offering plate for the construction of macadamized roads leading to the mission. He even had an Oldsmobile touring car that was in need of parts parked behind the church, and its eventual repair was something else he prayed for every night.

"We shall have the roads soon, Anton. Wait and see," said the priest. "The committee is making real progress. The governor sits on the board now."

We let the priest drive the truck up and down the road leading to Santa Fe. His hands and feet were well coordinated, and he never once missed a gear shift. A gasp of awe came from his mouth when he first used the air brakes.

He drove for more than an hour, laughing like a child, filling Mr. Westgard in on the progress of the Good Roads committee. When he finally parked the truck in front of the church, he made the sign of the cross, looked at Mr. Westgard in sudden solemnity, and said:

"Son, you are driving a miracle."

"... so you have made it, Mr. Westgard."

Santa Fe was like nothing I had seen before. It was the capital of the territory of New Mexico, and when we arrived, there were people travelling everywhere—on stagecoaches, horseback, prairie schooners. There were even some automobiles out on the street with us.

It wasn't just the size that surprised me—although it was by far the largest settlement we had seen since leaving Denver—it was also the city itself. I found out later that Santa Fe was the second oldest city in the United States. Only a place called St. Augustine, in Florida, which was settled by the Spanish in the late-sixteenth century, was older. It occurred to me as we made our way slowly down the congested streets that I had never seen a Spanish city before.

There were adobe buildings everywhere. Not the lonely, isolated buildings we had seen for the past several days, but hundreds of them, a city full of them. Mr. Westgard showed me the adobe building with the 700 apartments, and even with it standing right in front of me, I still had trouble believing it.

There were statues of Spanish governors and Catholic saints on just about every corner. There must have been a dozen St. Francis of Assisi statues alone. There were courtyard water fountains and boxes filled with brightly flowering plants hanging from the windows. The Sangre de Cristo Mountains were pushed up right close to the city, and a lazy brown river, the Santa Fe, cut through the middle.

The entire city flowed in every direction from a large central plaza we had trouble reaching because the connecting streets were so narrow. We circled around for more than an hour until we finally found a street we could get down. Then, when we reached the plaza, I almost crashed the truck, so distracted was I by the beauty of the buildings. There was the territorial capital building, the Palace of the Governors, and a basilica as large as any I had ever seen in Quebec, surrounded by scores of statues. The water fountain in the middle of the plaza was as large as a two-storey house, and the gurgling water so loud it reminded me of white-water rapids back home.

THE PIONEER FREIGHTER, MAKING ITS WAY TOWARDS SANTA FE.

We parked the truck in a garage next to the St. Francis Hotel where we would be staying for the next two nights. When we walked into the lobby with our dusty satchels and red-clay-stained clothes, I thought we would be asked to leave. It was beautiful and grand; the men in the lobby wore three-piece suits and the women all wore gowns even though it was mid-afternoon. I feared, for a minute, that we would be escorted off the premises, when a prosperous-looking man in a black, three-piece suit came up to us. But instead of throwing us out, he walked over to Mr. Westgard and extended his hand.

"So you have made it, Mr. Westgard. What did you think of our new macadamized roads?"

"A great improvement, Governor," answered Mr. Westgard. "A pity, though, that they seem to ring only Santa Fe."

"Just the beginning, Mr. Westgard. Come, there are some people I would like you to meet."

William Mills was the last territorial governor of New Mexico, and I have to admit, I was rather impressed that he was there in the hotel lobby waiting to greet Mr. Westgard. As our journey continued, I soon realized that the attention paid Mr. Westgard by important officials was a regular occurrence. As a prominent member of the Good Roads Movement, Mr. Westgard was a man whose favour was courted and curried by politicians of all stripes.

That's because after each of Mr. Westgard's road trips, he would submit a report to the federal government on the state of the nation's roads—the department of agriculture at first, then the office of public roads after it was created. He would also file reports with the various motoring associations, newspapers, and magazines.

A lot of towns in Colorado, New Mexico, and Arizona got stiffed when the railways came through in the last century, the railway engineers skipping over a town if they could save money by going in a different direction. The railways were arrogant and figured towns in the Southwest should come to the rail line, not the other way around. It's what happened to Las Vegas. It even happened to Santa Fe—the Atchison, Topeka and Santa Fe Railway never went to Santa Fe, opting instead to pass south of the city, which may still annoy the citizens of Santa Fe.

So there were always people waiting to meet Mr. Westgard to make sure the same thing didn't happen again when the new horseless-carriage roads were built. Mr. Westgard loved the attention. When we would resume our journey, the first hour or so would always be a retelling of the meeting he had had with the governor or the mayor, a meeting in which Mr. Westgard was always clever and knowledgeable, and the assembled politicians were always fawning and ignorant.

I left Mr. Westgard and Mr. Thompson in the lobby of the hotel, speaking to the governor, and went to my room. It was a large room with a window overlooking the courtyard. I stared at another horseless carriage trying to make its way down a side street, the driver finally giving up and putting the car into reverse. This was not going to be an easy city to get around in, no matter where the roads were built.

We stayed in Santa Fe to get more gasoline and oil, more fresh food, to give Mr. Thompson and Mr. Westgard time to send their telegrams, and me a chance to mail some postcards. I decided not to mail my postcards from the lobby of the hotel but to go, instead, for a walk and mail them from the post office. I travelled down the narrow streets of Santa Fe and got jostled about in the crowds. A great many of the women were dark haired and beautiful, their beauty not hidden behind the lace scarves they wore around their heads. The men wore short jackets with sequins sown on the lapels or around the pockets.

Most of the towns and cities I had visited in the United States were not that different from towns and cities in Canada. Some were larger than where I grew up; some, like Denver, were so beautiful they took your breath away; some, like Las Vegas, made you think about the bad days of the Wild West. But Santa Fe was the first place I had seen where it seemed I had fallen asleep in one place and woken up halfway around the world.

Albuquerque and the Rio Grande

When we left Santa Fe two days later, Mr. Westgard told me about his meeting with Governor Mills.

"The governor said he was so embarrassed by my last report, he had personally started a campaign to improve the roads in the territory."

"What did you say in your last report?" I asked.

"I reported the truth, Mr. MacLean, that Bernalillo County contained the worst roads of any part of the transcontinental route down the Santa Fe Trail."

I was surprised someone who had just been so insulted would be glad to see the insulter as Governor Mills seemed to be when Mr. Westgard arrived at the St. Francis Hotel. Yet there was always something about politics I never quite grasped, so I didn't spend much time worrying about it.

"He told me 10,000 dollars had been raised just to improve the roads in that one county. That I would notice many improvements as we made our way to Albuquerque."

We were driving down a switchback as Mr. Westgard spoke, the grade so steep it was like we were driving in circles. There were many dormant volcanoes around Santa Fe, all of them eroded down to nothing more than tall hills, and our route took us over lava rock, which is rock left over when a volcano has blown. The rock was coarse and brittle, and I worried about the Goodrich tires, but they held up fine.

"It was a most productive meeting," Mr. Westgard continued, "even though there was one gentleman there—I gather he owns a livery in Santa Fe—who expressed the opinion that automobiles are merely a passing fad. That the governor is wasting his time joining the various Good Roads committees."

Mr. Westgard snorted in amusement. The people in this territory still needed to be educated. It was a lucky thing for them he was around to help.

"I pointed out to this gentleman that the first automobile was manufactured in the United States not much more than fifteen years ago and already there are hundreds of thousands of them on the streets of America, getting faster and more durable with each passing year.

BOULDERS WERE COMMON OBSTACLES ON THE ROADS IN 1911.

"That is not a fad, I told the gentleman. That is the future."

Mr. Thompson laughed. Calling his father's business a fad probably didn't sit well with him, either. It sounded like Mr. Westgard had done a fine job of putting the livery owner in his place.

The truck ran nice and smooth that day as we made our way up and down the stumps of old volcanoes; we never got past third gear, but there were few arroyos and irrigation ditches to contend with, and we made good time.

For the next three days, we made our way toward Albuquerque, the largest town in the New Mexican territory. According to Mr. West-gard, we were now travelling on another historic trail, this one called the El Camino Real.

"Travel that way for 1,600 miles," he said, pointing south, "and you will be in Mexico City."

Camino Real means royal road in Spanish, and this trail had been around a lot longer than the Santa Fe Trail. It was the old trade

A SWITCHBACK ON THE WAY TO ALBUQUERQUE.

route for the Spanish and Pueblo Indians; many of the adobe homes we passed were several centuries old. I wasn't used to anything being that old unless it was a white pine, and I stared at the homes in wonder. My childhood home of Campbell's Bay had been around for all of seventy years. Most of the dishes inside the adobe dwellings were older than any house I had walked into as a kid.

I couldn't get used to the countryside we were travelling through, either. Every hour of the day brought some new surprise. We'd crest a hill, and there at the bottom of a canyon would be a Douglas fir or some sort of maple. Or we would be travelling over red clay and lava rock when we rounded a bend, and suddenly, there in front of us would be a swamp. That happened right outside Santa Fe on our first day, Mr. Westgard calling the swamp La Cienega, which meant stream. Sure enough, there was a stream with willows and dogwoods growing beside it and brightly coloured flowers I had never seen before. Only two miles back was some of the most barren, desolate land you could imagine.

We drove through La Cienega and San Felipe Pueblo, making our way toward Algodones and Bernalillo County, driving over some fine macadamized roads the closer we got to Bernalillo. But it was still slow going. We had to repair, or outright replace, seventeen bridges around Algodones alone.

"It seems," said Mr. Westgard, "that the governor's fine work has not taken into account the weight of a motorized cargo vehicle."

It was tedious work although we all pitched in, and I think the three of us were getting to be pretty good carpenters. The stack of lumber in the back of the truck was starting to noticeably shrink, and Mr. Westgard said we might need to get some more in Albuquerque. I didn't know how much oak planking would cost in the territory, but oak was one tree I hadn't seen yet. Mr. Westgard made a joke about Mr. Thompson wiring his dad for more money.

"Tell him we are building bridges as we go. The roads might belong to the Saurer Motor Truck Company by the time we are finished."

As we got closer to Albuquerque, we passed many fine-looking homes—haciendas—with what looked like vineyards growing around them, which I had trouble believing even after Mr. Westgard told me that's exactly what they were. The Spanish had planted grapes back in the sixteenth century, and while much of the work had been a waste of time, the vines grew quite well in Bernalillo County, which was a fertile valley.

Then, later in the day, I thought my eyes were playing tricks on me again when the blue horizon in front of us started to break apart. Fracture. Become two different things. The more we travelled, the more pronounced it became—blue sky separated from blue ground—until finally I turned to Mr. Westgard and said, "Is that a river?"

"The Rio Grande," he replied.

We hooked up with the river and drove beside it until we reached Albuquerque. When we reached the Alvarado Hotel, the mayor was waiting for us, along with the man who headed up the Albuquerque Chamber of Commerce and a reporter from the *Albuquerque Morning Journal*.

It had taken us three weeks to drive from Denver to the Alvarado Hotel, a distance of 447 miles. Our average speed had been 3.26 miles per hour.

A Traffic Block in the Southwest

The next morning we arose early as our bodies were getting accustomed to that sort of daily routine, and had breakfast in the dining room of the Alvarado. Mr. Thompson had business to do, sending off telegrams to Chicago and New York and meeting another man his father had been in contact with, this one a dry goods merchant who might be in need of a truck. Mr. Thompson said he would talk to the man first before bringing me along.

When he left, Mr. Westgard and I sat in silence for a minute. That didn't last long: Mr. Westgard could not sit still for any length of time nor could he leave a man sitting near him without assisting that man by giving him some direction in life.

"Mr. MacLean, I think we should inspect the truck," he said after we had finished our coffee. "There will be some tough going in the next few weeks."

With that, we went to the garage next to the Alvarado where, much to our surprise, we discovered several automobiles had arrived overnight. Men in ankle-length motoring coats were milling around the cars, and Mr. West-gard muttered under his breath that if everyone tried to leave at the same time there would be one "miserable traffic block."

I had never heard the phrase before, and Mr. Westgard said there shouldn't be a need to use such a phrase in Albuquerque, never thought he would see the day when he needed to use it in the Southwest. He went on to say a traffic block meant people and vehicles all coming and going at the same time—so many people and vehicles coming and going at the same time, no one actually came and went anywhere.

"Traffic block?"

"That's right, Mr. MacLean, traffic block, from the French, trafique. What we have here this morning, I am afraid, is a traffic block."

One car quickly caught Mr. Westgard's attention. It was a strange-looking car with an enclosed body, something I had never seen before. Two men were standing beside it, loading bedrolls and satchels into the covered back seat.

"Mr. McGready!" said Mr. Westgard as he walked toward the car.

A GRAND ADVENTURE

A TRAFFIC "BLOCK" IN THE AMERICAN SOUTHWEST, SPRING OF 1911.

"Mr. Westgard!" said one of the men, as he turned around. They shook hands warmly, and then the man said, "What brings you to Albuquerque at this time of year?"

"A commission with the Saurer Motor Truck Company and the Office of Public Roads," replied Mr. Westgard with obvious pride. "I am taking a truck across these glorious states of ours to see if such a feat may be accomplished. And you, Mr. McGready, what brings you to Albuquerque?"

"Oh, just a short excursion in my new Cadillac. It is the Model 30 Touring Car. Allow me to introduce my driver, Mr. Frederick Fisher. Mr. Fisher, this is Mr. Westgard, a pathfinder of some repute."

I knew what was coming next, and even before Mr. Westgard had started shaking the young man's hand, I had begun moving up behind him so that when Mr. Westgard turned around I was standing right there.

"Allow me to introduce my driver, Mr. George MacLean, from New York City."

I reached out my hand, and the man called Mr. McGready shook it firmly.

"New York City, you say? You're a long way from home, young man. How did you hook up with this scoundrel you're travelling with?"

"I work for the truck company," I said, and this answer seemed to satisfy him greatly for he turned immediately away from me and resumed talking to Mr. Westgard.

"A truck trip across the United States. From ocean to ocean?"

"Indeed."

"Has such a thing been done before?"

"It has not. The Saurer Pioneer Freighter shall be the first truck to accomplish the feat."

Mr. McGready nodded his head a little and then said, "Well, good luck to you, Mr. Westgard. I am on my way back to Los Angeles. Perhaps we shall see each other out on the road."

With that, he turned and climbed into the passenger side of the fancy car with the covered cab. His driver climbed behind the wheel next to him and fired the magneto ignition, so the engine started nice and smooth. Then, with a wave of Mr. McGready's hand, they left the garage.

Mr. Westgard told me later that Mr. McGready was a wealthy industrialist from Los Angeles, who fashioned himself a pathfinder, even though, Mr. Westgard was quick to inform me, Mr. McGready had never travelled a single mile in an automobile that Mr. Westgard had not mapped first.

"Cadillac," said Mr. Westgard as we watched the car leave the garage. "Can't say I have ever cared for that name. They shall have to change it one day."

That wasn't the only car that caught Mr. Westgard's attention that morning. Parked two stalls over from our truck was a seven-passenger car with an American flag flying from one staff of the overhead roof.

"My goodness," said Mr. Westgard, upon seeing the car. "What has brought the Pathfinder to Albuquerque?"

He was speaking to himself, or to me, perhaps, for I was standing close enough to him, but it was a man walking up behind us who answered:

"We are going to Mexico, Anton. Care to accompany us?"

We both turned to see a chubby man dressed in a long whale-skin coat, goggles covering his eyes, striding up to us and extending his hand to Mr. Westgard.

"Lattis, as I live and breathe."

The men shook hands and then briefly embraced, which surprised me, for I had never seen Mr. Westgard do such a thing, with the exception of the priest at the San Miguel Mission.

"Mr. MacLean, let me introduce you to Mr. Lattis Schwasche, a fellow member of the Touring Club of America."

I shook the man's hand while Mr. Westgard kept on talking.

"Are you taking good care of her, Lattis? I shall want her back one day."

Lattis laughed and said, "She will be waiting for you in New York, Anton, later this summer."

As the men talked, I figured out Mr. Schwasche's car was the same one Mr.

A GRAND ADVENTURE

MANY MILES YET TO GO.

Westgard had used the year before to travel to Los Angeles—the Premier Pathfinder. I had heard many stories of the car: how well it performed; how the Premier Automobile Company of Indianapolis designed fast and rugged cars that did well not only on the race track but also on the mountains and deserts of the Southwest; how Mr. Westgard loved this car so much he had even given it a name—the Pathfinder.

"This is the first I am hearing of a trip to Mexico," I heard Mr. Westgard say. "I thought you were taking the Pathfinder on the Midland Trail later this spring."

"We still are, Anton. But we shall do it west to east after arriving in Los Angeles.

We changed our plans shortly after shipping the Pathfinder west. Someone at the monthly meeting pointed out that there has never been an American automobile journey through Mexico."

You could tell from the expression on Mr. Westgard's face that if there were a first to be had in the Premier Pathfinder—like taking her to Mexico—it should be his, not his friend's. What came out of his mouth, though, was:

"Is there not an insurrection under way at the present time in Mexico?"

To which Mr. Schwasche laughed and replied, "My dear Anton, when isn't there an insurrection under way in Mexico?"

"Except for being scalped, I think we are much the same."

Mr. Schwasche and his driver left the garage shortly afterward, Mr. Westgard looking all far-eyed and miserable when the car pulled away. Mr. Thompson and I met Lattis Schwasche in Los Angeles later that summer, and it turned out he did indeed have some problems in Mexico because of Pancho Villa and his revolutionaries: troubles crossing the border, with the Americans thinking they must have been gun-runners; then troubles with the Mexicans, who thought they must have been spies, when the got across. He seemed mighty glad to be back in the United States when we met him. (I doubt if that story would have cheered Mr. Westgard any even if he had been around to hear it. The man never minded adversity, and I could tell by the way he looked at the car when it left Albuquerque that he was mighty possessive about it. Heck, he talked about that car more than he talked about his family.)

Maybe it was the car that got him thinking about it, but, as I started my inspection, Mr. Westgard began talking about being a path-finder and how he fell into such a vocation.

"I became a pathfinder while working for the American cavalry," he said, my head now under the hood checking the motor. "I was hired as a surveyor, but it wasn't long before I found my true calling in life. It is a wonderful thing when that happens, Mr. MacLean. A wonderful thing."

Mr. Westgard went on to say that, after spending a few years doing mapping and surveying work for the federal government, the car manufacturers came calling, offering him their latest models to test drive, to take them out for transcontinental runs or city-to-city races, maybe write a little article for the automotive journals. He kept daily journals of his new travels. Bought a camera so he could take photographs of everything he saw, the same way he used to record addresses and landmarks for the Century Map Company of Philadelphia. Somewhere along the line, he started calling himself a pathfinder.

"I think the appellation is quite accurate," he said as I checked the ball bearings, seeing that not even those were damaged. "This in no way diminishes the heroic deeds of our original pathfinders, the brave men of Colonial times. I would not wish you to think such a thing.

"I also grant you, quite readily, that I never had to deal with hostile Indians as our original pathfinders did nor am I ever denied the protection and comfort of civilized men to pass my nights with. Why, even at the roughest of mining camps, even in the wildest of terrains, one can usually find civilized people travelling to and fro these days."

At this point, he paused to look around the garage, took a few steps forward then a few steps back, like an actor looking for his spot on the stage. He often did this, and I wondered for a moment if I would hear the same stories if I ever made another road trip with him.

"Yet it seems to me," he continued, having found a spot to his liking, "that the similarities in our professional lives are far more striking than the differences.

"The original pathfinders came west to cut paths for the horse-drawn wagons, stagecoaches, and settlers that would follow. I also came west, only I cut paths for the horseless carriage; for the tourists, businessmen, and adventurers who would follow me.

"All in all, except for being scalped, I think we are much the same."

A Dangerous Crossing

I finished the inspection and told Mr. Westgard that the Pioneer Freighter was in tip-top shape, didn't even need ball bearings. Gasoline and oil—that's all she needed; that was all she ever needed. Satisfied with my report, he left me in the garage and headed back to the Alvarado where Mr. Thompson should have returned from his errands. Before leaving the garage, I took another look under the hood of the truck, fearing for a moment I must have missed something, not understanding how any horseless carriage could have gone through what the Pioneer Freighter had just gone through and not have damages somewhere.

I still didn't find anything amiss, so I closed the hood and went away in a happy mood, already looking forward to taking the truck back on the road the next morning. I had never driven this much before, and it was a strange sensation, driving night and day, getting by on five hours sleep, sometimes turning the day on its head, so you slept in the heat of the afternoon and travelled by night.

Some days we were fast, averaging nearly fifteen miles an hour. Other days we would spend seven hours just to travel a mile, laying down a corduroy road in order to get over a mudhole, or using the winch to ford some river that didn't have a ferry. Strange thing was, none of it seemed that different after a while; slow or fast, hard work or easy, it all seemed part of the same thing.

There was the same sense of excitement when I saw the truck in the morning. The same light-headedness when I turned the magneto ignition, and the engine started nice and smart. Didn't matter where we were on a map or how difficult the day before had been.

I thought I had driven plenty before I came to Denver and met Mr. Westgard. I had driven trucks and automobiles up and down the Northeastern Seaboard, made deliveries for the T. Eaton Company to every borough in Toronto, but this trip was different. My destination was so far away I couldn't even think in terms of a destination as something final and looming. It almost didn't matter if I made it. Just moving somewhere, moving anywhere, was starting to be enough for me.

Moving as not a destination thing or a daily

thing, but as an every thing—that was new to me. The more I did it, the more I wanted it. Like I was some sort of hop head or some bad-case drunkard, the kind the temperance ladies warned you about; the ones they were petitioning the American government to save from themselves. From their wicked, self-indulgent selves.

If I weren't having so much fun, I would be getting worried.

We left Albuquerque on March 25, Mr. Westgard speaking to a reporter from the *Albuquerque Morning Journal* before we left the Alvarado. The reporter asked when he expected to be in Phoenix; Mr. Westgard told the old man that he had asked a difficult question, but he could guarantee him we would be there when we arrived.

There he was again, not giving a direct answer to a direct question. Like he was afraid of numbers or something.

Our route was going to take us to San Antonio where Mr. Westgard said we would cross the Rio Grande River by way of a railway bridge. This was going out of our way, but Mr. Westgard said the direct route to Phoenix would be bad this time of year, perhaps even impassable, so this was the best way to go.

We drove beside the Rio Grande for most of the day, and I have to admit, I didn't understand the name. The river back home, the Ottawa, was a heck of a lot more majestic than the Rio Grande. The Ottawa was a wide river with a fast-moving current and steamboats that made their way back and forth from Montreal or down the Rideau Canal, which emptied into the Ottawa. There was no way the Rio Grande River could handle a steamboat. It was the sort of thing you canoed down. I looked around at the buttes, the high mesas, and they crowded in on the river, made it look small, the way the land never did to a major river back home.

For most of that day, an eagle flew high above us as if we were being tracked, until finally it flew off just before sunset. After that, a strong wind came whistling down from the San Cristo Mountains, sending rippling patterns across the surface of the Rio Grande. We watched until night came, each of us quiet and lost in our own thoughts, perhaps imagining what the patterns most resembled.

For the next three days, we drove through the Carthage coal mines, the Rio Grande dipping in and out of sight. When we reached San Antonio, we stayed in a hotel for the night and, early the next morning, reached the train bridge over the river. I looked at that bridge. While it is not my custom to ask many questions of any man I work for, I couldn't help myself.

"Are you sure about this, Mr. Westgard?" I asked before I could stop myself.

Mr. Westgard looked at me as if I had just punched him in the stomach.

"Mr. MacLean, I have done this many

THE PIONEER FREIGHTER RIDING THE RAILS.

times in the past. You must trust me."

I looked at the bridge again and found myself wondering how many people in this world checked out of this life with "You must trust me" being the last words they ever heard. The bridge was high—maybe a quarter-mile or so above the river—and it was long. The track on the other side rounded a mesa almost immediately; if a Denver and Rio Grande train was heading east at the same time as we set out across the bridge, we were done for. Even Mr. Thompson, who had gone along with all of Mr. Westgard's instructions so far, seemed a little pale in the face while looking at the bridge.

This was more than a leap of faith. This was a swan dive.

"How can you be sure a train isn't coming?" I asked.

"No eastbound trains are scheduled for another hour," said Mr. Westgard. "I looked at the schedules before we left San Antonio.

"Besides," he continued, "the engineers sound the whistle when they approach this bridge for exactly the reason that is now worrying you. People often use the bridge. The engineers are aware of this. The whistle is always sounded."

I looked again at the bridge.

"What do we do if we hear a whistle?"

"I believe our truck has a reverse gear, does it not?"

I didn't dare look at the man. Backing up on the bridge with a train bearing down on us. This was his plan? Still, I had little choice in the matter. Mr. Westgard was determined to cross the Rio Grande by way of this train bridge, and unless Mr. Thompson and I mutinied, that's what we were going to do. We might as well get it over with as soon as possible.

When we were one hundred feet across the bridge, we heard the whistle. I was driving the truck at an angle, one set of back tires on the steel girder, the other on the ties. When the whistle sounded, we looked at each other in surprise, having convinced ourselves the Good Lord would reward our heroism. Instead, we were going to be cast aside for the fools we were.

We still hadn't seen the train, only heard the whistle, and for a moment, I considered following Mr. Westgard's suggestion — put the truck into reverse and get out of there as quick as we could. I don't know why I stepped on the gas pedal instead.

"Mr. MacLean!" screamed Mr. Westgard.

Right. That was why. If the man had been wrong about the train, maybe he was wrong about going in reverse, too. Why check out of this world following the advice of another man? Might as well be your call.

I tore down the tracks, shifting into third

gear, then fourth, then I saw the train coming around the bend, looking for all the world like some angry metal monster spitting steam and dust. We could hear the engineer hit the brakes, the harsh sound of metal grinding on metal. We could see sparks spitting from the steel wheels. See the outside pistons lock.

One thing we didn't see was the train slowing down.

The truck was almost tipping over now, careening out of control, running at a crazy angle down the rail line. There was nothing I could do to correct it. There wasn't time. I kept my foot pushed on the gas pedal, hoping I hadn't misjudged the distance to the other side of the bridge.

I don't think there was more than twenty feet between us when we reached the other side of the Rio Grande. I gave the steering wheel a hard crank to the right, praying we wouldn't tip or get trapped on the steel girder.

We could feel the train as it passed. A rush of hot air against our cheeks as if a boiler room door had suddenly opened beside us. The truck shook and then fell still. None of us looked behind. Just stared straight ahead at the now deserted rail line.

For several minutes, we said nothing. Just stared at the rail line ahead of us, listening to the train to Albuquerque retreat into the distance. Finally, Mr. Westgard said:

"I've never known a train to be that far ahead of schedule."

Camp Mormon and
Another Truck Demonstration

You'd think if a man nearly killed you, he might apologize for it. And if he genuinely weren't sorry, then maybe he would at least be embarrassed and do the things an embarrassed man does—avoid eye contact, keep his thoughts to himself, look for some sort of hole to crawl into, so he couldn't kill again that day.

But being sorry or embarrassed wasn't in Mr. Westgard's nature. So for the next hour, he complained about the shoddy scheduling of the Denver and Rio Grande Western Railway company. Said he was seriously considering registering a complaint. Like it was the railway company's fault they were sending a train down their track. Mr. Westgard eventually decided a complaint was definitely required to protect against such a "mishap" occurring again. With this out of the way, he began to talk of other things, a change of subject for which I was grateful.

"There are some interesting mining camps ahead of us, Mr. Thompson," he said.

I don't think Mr. Thompson felt like talking yet because he didn't answer right away. He still looked pale. I wondered for a moment if he were going to be sick.

"Perhaps as we make our way to Arizona you will find a camp that will purchase one of your trucks," Mr. Westgard continued cheerfully. "I certainly believe the iron ore camps could use your fine product."

This seemed to cheer up Mr. Thompson slightly for he finally said: "Yes, perhaps I will make a sale. At least I am alive and can attempt such a transaction."

If this was intended as a criticism of Mr. Westgard, the man gave no indication of twigging to it: he just pulled a map from his satchel and started to show Mr. Thompson some of the camps where he might have success.

In the next few days, we came to understand what Mr. Westgard had meant by "some interesting camps." Pulling into the mining camps in Western New Mexico and Eastern Arizona was like pulling into foreign countries, all the miners being immigrants to these glorious

A MEXICAN VILLAGE IN NEW MEXICO.

states of ours, each camp tending to allow its own kind to work there and no others. There were German camps, with tough, bearded men dressed in leather britches. Russian camps, with cabbage burning in cook pots all day, so you could smell the camps many miles before you reached them.

There was even a Mormon camp. (Mr. Westgard explained that the Mormon religion was popular in the West, particularly in Utah.) In this camp, the men had long hair, full beards, and there were many women and children living in adobe huts not far from the mine, which was unusual for a mining camp as most of them housed only men.

Mr. Thompson gave his regular truck demonstration at Camp Mormon, but this was dif-

ferent as well because there was no drinking, no giddy run on the truck to a nearby still. The miners understood English, so they listened to what Mr. Thompson had to say, inspected the truck thoroughly, handled the pamphlets he proffered carefully, not shoving them into their pockets the way the other miners did.

"The tonnage on this truck right now, you say it is 17,000 pounds, Mr. Thompson?" one of the Mormon miners asked, and you could tell Mr. Thompson was pleased not only with the question but also with the fact the man could pronounce his name.

"It was 17,000 pounds when we departed Denver. We have used some wood since then, but we are still carrying a payload of around 5,000 pounds."

"And your speed on the trip, Mr. Thompson, how does it compare to a commercial dray?"

"Well, the speed is an interesting factor to calculate"—you could tell Mr. Thompson didn't like this question as much—"On certain days during the trip, we have averaged more than ten miles an hour consistently through the day, a rate of speed no commercial dray could ever hope to reach or maintain."

"And on other days?"

"Well, on other days, there have been no roads to speak of, a condition we do not expect will last much longer in this country. On those days it has been"—here Mr. Thompson stopped and searched for the right word. What might it be? Oh, right—"slower."

"Slower?"

"Yes, somewhat slower."

The Mormon miners still seemed interested even after this admission. I must have taken everyone in the camp for a drive, even the women and children, although we left camp the next morning without a sale. This did not seem to discourage Mr. Thompson in the slightest; he was now eager to telegram his father with the news that Mormons like trucks.

"How many Mormons did you say were in the Southwest?" he asked Mr. Westgard.

"A great many. In Utah, most of the state is Mormon."

"Utah. My father will need to contact someone there. Salt Lake City is the capital, correct?"

"That's correct."

For the rest of that day, Mr. Thompson was perhaps the happiest I had seen him on the trip, asking all sorts of questions about Utah and Mormons.

Crossing the Continental Divide

Years later, I came upon a postcard I had purchased in Albuquerque and never mailed, intending I suppose to post it from Phoenix. On the back of the postcard, I had written down an itinerary of our trip out of Albuquerque, recording the dates, the weather, and where we camped every night. The postcard read like this:

March 25 — left Albuquerque for Camp Adobe, 24.5 miles, 9 hours in transit.

March 26 — Camp Adobe to Camp Rincon, 9.25 hours in transit, clear, sandy, and rutty.

March 27 — stayed in Camp Rincon.

March 28 — Camp Rincon to Camp Ojo la Llama, 28 miles, 10.30 hours in transit.

March 29 — Camp Ojo la Llama to San Antonio, 22.5 miles, 9.15 hours in transit, rough road through Carthage coal mines.

March 30 — San Antonio to Socorro, 11.2 miles, 2 hours in transit, rough going through Blue Canyon.

March 31 — Socorro to Magdalena. 29.1 miles, 8.35 hours in transit, steep and narrow through Letimar Canyon.

Maybe I forgot to mail the postcard. Or maybe when we reached Phoenix I decided it did such a poor job of describing the trip from Albuquerque, I would have been lying to whomever I sent it. I remember that part of the road trip well. How the truck kept climbing its way through the snow of the White Mountains, not even following a trail most days. The journey was more like bushwhacking: having a rough idea which direction we needed to go in and heading that way, hoping the obstacles in front of us—which we had to find a way of bypassing—wouldn't throw us too far off course.

The snow hid boulders, fallen trees, ravines, and I think we hit every one. The truck would suddenly lurch up or fall down like some wooden roller coaster at a county fair. Once we hit a boulder so hard, the steering wheel was rammed into my chest, taking away my breath and making me momentarily lose control.

We kept going. Often, Mr. Westgard and

SNOW AND MORE SNOW AS THE PIONEER FREIGHTER APPROACHES THE CONTINENTAL DIVIDE.

Mr. Thompson walked beside the truck to help push when the snow got too deep. We had good warm clothing, but still we shivered, the wind whipping down the mountain and stinging our faces as it found its way under our heavy coats and up our trousers.

I had to take my gloves off quite regularly to adjust the chains on the tires, and at the end of one day, my fingertips had white dots splayed across them. I worried that night about frostbite, could barely sleep because of it, knowing plenty of men back home who had lost fingers and toes to frostbite while working in the lumber camps. But the next morning, the spots were gone, and I relaxed somewhat.

As we made our way, we kept track of our altitude by referring to Mr. Westgard's topographical maps. Nine thousand feet. Nine thousand, five hundred. Ten thousand. On the day we hit ten thousand, I wondered how many motor cars had been that high.

Even with the chains, lumber, and two men pushing the truck when she got stuck, we were making the slowest time of the trip. We drove nine to ten hours a day and then had to set up camp. On several nights, we were so tired we didn't even bother with a cook fire or a tent; just rolled ourselves into our bedrolls and went to sleep under the truck.

We kept going. Past frozen creeks, snow-covered cedars and junipers, abandoned mine shafts, and empty trapping cabins. We spent a night in one such cabin, grateful to be out of the wind and the snow, sleeping in tiny bunks built into the walls. Although mining camps were marked on our maps, many of them were abandoned. Maybe until the snowstorms stopped. Maybe forever. We were never sure.

The work tired us out and made us silent. We didn't talk to each other. Just bore down on what needed to be done. I don't believe I have ever been so single-minded in my life, so oblivious to the people and things around me. It was just me, a truck, and a mountain range that was refusing to be crossed. There was nothing else left in the world.

Even Mr. Thompson, who had not complained once on our journey, seemed to be getting worn down. "George, I've never been so cold," he said to me one night, and I was genuinely worried for him. By this time, we had travelled plenty of rough miles over country I wouldn't have thought existed before I'd seen it—canyons, switchbacks, lava rock, carbon rock, quicksand, more lava rock, then some mud, then different kinds of rocks. We had travelled through rainstorms, sand storms, snowstorms, but it wasn't until we reached the White Mountains that the thought entered my head—"We might not make it. This is as far as we're going to be able to go."

Instead of saying this to Mr. Thompson when he complained of the cold, I said, "We're going to be fine. Mr. Westgard knows the way."

We kept going. Ten thousand, one hundred feet. Ten thousand, two hundred. Ten thousand, four hundred, the truck now climbing at a 30 percent grade. The air around us was thin and cold, and for not a moment of those days, were we warm, the cold now so deep in our bones, it was like another layer of marrow had been added; a frigid, keep-you-drowsy-all-day piece of marrow.

On most of our days up until then, we had met other people while travelling on the road: miners, ranchers, Indians, soldiers, other travellers, but as we made our way up the eastern flank of the White Mountains, there was no one. Only at the camps did we find people. No one was bothering with the roads at this time of year. It was the one time on the trip when I really did feel like a pathfinder. Felt that if the truck rolled on us and we died, it would be a long time before anyone found our bodies.

Then one morning as Mr. Thompson and I tried to warm ourselves around a cook fire, Mr. Westgard kept himself busy checking his compass against one of his topographical maps. He laid the compass on the map, took a pencil, and drew a line. Moved the compass to another spot on the map, triangulated a line with the one he had already drawn. Repeated the operation several times as we stared at him.

Finally, he brought the map over to the cook fire and sat beside us. He pointed with his finger to where the lines crossed and where he had marked a large X. The circular lines on the map said we had fallen to ten thousand, one hundred feet.

And just like that we were over the Continental Divide.

A River Crossing at Fort Apache

On April 12, as we began our descent down the White Mountains and the western flank of the Continental Divide, we crossed the territorial boundary between New Mexico and Arizona. It had taken us twenty-seven days to drive across New Mexico. We had travelled 434 miles.

From where we reached the bottom of the White Mountains, there was a direct route to Phoenix, but we didn't take it. Several times on the journey, we had to make detours like this, so Mr. Westgard could do some of his work for the Office of Public Roads. This time he had to inspect the roads leading to Fort Apache.

That ended up being a funny story because there were plenty of people who helped us on our journey across the United States. Ranchers would put us up for the night, miners would feed us, and farmers would pull us out of sinkholes using their mules and occasionally even their oxen (though some of them wanted to be paid for the service). Only once, though, did we have to call out the cavalry. That happened at Fort Apache.

Fort Apache was in the heart of Apache country, the "real Wild West," as Mr. West-gard liked to call it. This was where Cochise and Geronimo and other Indian leaders once fought the American government, and as we made our way toward the fort, I could well understand the difficulty the government had in capturing them. The country here was a wild maze of buttes, foothills, and hidden ravines; land that could hide a war party almost anywhere, and you would never know it was there—could march right beside it and never be the wiser.

We reached Fort Apache after four days of hard driving across such land and were given a warm welcome by the soldiers, many of whom had never seen a truck. That night, we dined with the commanding officer of the fort. Shortly into our dinner, the officer told us we should get used to military life because we would be his guests for a while. He went on to explain that the Black River had flooded its banks several days before and showed no sign of receding any time soon. Why, he had

SOME FRIENDS FROM FORT APACHE, MANY OF WHOM HAD NEVER SEEN A TRUCK.

Barbara Arnott

a company of soldiers marooned on the other side of the river that had been camped there for nearly a week.

We were disappointed to hear this as you might imagine. We had been making painfully slow time for nearly three weeks and were not anxious for any more delays. As the commanding officer explained the difficulties he was having with the Black River, Mr. Westgard seemed to be lost in thought. When the officer had finished talking, Mr. Westgard said he might have a solution to the problem of the marooned soldiers, a solution that would solve our problems at the same time.

"If you can lend me a company of cavalrymen, twenty stout men with brave hearts, I think I can get your soldiers home," he said.

"How?" the officer asked.

"By using the Pioneer Freighter."

"Your truck?"

"Yes. If you can help us get the truck across the river, I can guarantee you that we will get your soldiers home."

The officer was intrigued by the proposition and told Mr. Westgard he could have his company of cavalrymen. He suggested we meet the company at the point down river—it was about twenty miles south of the fort—where the soldiers were marooned.

The next morning, we set off bright and early, which was not a problem as we were jarred from our beds by a bugle calling reveille. This left us no choice but to arise and was enough, in itself, to discourage me from any thoughts of future military service. As we travelled beside the Black River, we soon understood the problem the soldiers were having. The river was running fast and strong and must have cleared her banks several days ago, then kept rising, because there were full-grown cottonwoods in the far channels on both sides.

The driving was slow as there was no trail to speak of running beside the river, but by late morning, we reached the point on the river where a company of cavalrymen was waiting. On the far shore, we could see the tents and covered wagons of the marooned soldiers.

Mr. Westgard's idea was to get a block and tackle line run across the Black River, after which the army wagons on the far shore could be pulled across using the winch on the truck to support them.

The plan required the truck to go first to lay the line, and as I drove the Pioneer Freighter into the fast-moving current of the river, I wasn't so much worried about being swept away—we weighed more than eight tons after all—as I was of hitting a boulder and capsizing. The water was moving so fast there was a white froth on the surface, and what lay beneath was anyone's guess.

I did indeed hit a boulder about half-way across, and the truck tilted precariously for a moment, the same angle it had been at when we crossed the train bridge over the Rio Grande. But it then slid off the boulder, corrected itself with a big splash, and I could hear cheers from cavalrymen on both sides of

the river. It seemed as though we were their entertainment for the afternoon, whether the river crossing was successful or not.

A lone cavalryman on horseback had crossed the river ahead of us, bringing a line he could attach to a mule team on the far shore. It was a good thing we had thought of this for the far bank had a 30 percent incline, and it took every ounce of strength from those mules to pull the Pioneer Freighter from the river.

Once we were back on dry land, there were more cheers and shouts from the cavalrymen. The block and tackle was then pulled tight across the river, and, with the team master holding onto the line in front of him while a line running from the rear of the wagon was attached to the winch on the truck, the covered wagons started making their way across the Black River.

By sunset, the operation was complete, and again there were cheers and yelps from the cavalrymen. We cheered along with them as best we could although by this time we were the only ones on the western bank of the river, and our celebration was a tame affair compared to the far shoreline.

The next morning—once again we were awoken by the bleating of a bugle—we waved goodbye to the cavalry. As we resumed our journey, I asked Mr. Westgard what he would write about Fort Apache in his report to the Office of Public Roads.

"Need bridge," he answered.

The Wild West and the Opening of the Roosevelt Dam

We made our way through the San Carlos Apache Reservation, the road we were travelling on little more than a stagecoach trail, and a bad one at that. The truck tilted and jumped like a spinning top; not a bone in our bodies was untested when we stopped to camp at the end of a day's journey. This was wild country where cattle rustlers and bandits still roamed, and our rifles were never far from our sides. Mr. Westgard had a Colt pistol as well, which he kept tucked in the crook of his back under the pleated army coat he wore every day.

The land around Fort Apache is where Ike and Phineas Clanton ran to hide after the gunfight at the OK Corral, a plan that didn't work well for the brothers because Ike was shot dead by a sheriff in Springerville, and Phineas got arrested shortly afterward for holding up a stagecoach. As a boy in Campbell's Bay, I had read books about the Clantons, their arch rivals, the Earps, and the gunfight at the OK Corral; read any story about the Wild West I could find. I had trouble some days believing I was driving across the same country those people once roamed.

It was here that the American government tried to put Geronimo onto a reservation even though he kept leaving and running down to Mexico. He was the last Apache to surrender. Whenever I played cowboys and Indians with my friends in Campbell's Bay, I was the only one who wanted to play the part of the Indians: I had read about Geronimo, though, and figured he was a tough old bird, probably knew the country better than anyone, so why wouldn't you want to be him?

A lot of those characters I read about as a kid were still around or hadn't been gone all that long. Geronimo was at Teddy Roosevelt's inauguration. Wyatt Earp was living in California. The Apache Kid, even he was supposed to be around somewhere. Or so the ranchers told us whenever we stopped to talk to them on our way to Phoenix. He had become famous as an Indian Scout, then, later, as a man accused of a murder he probably didn't commit. The injustice of that made the Kid so

TEDDY ROOSEVELT AT THE OPENING OF THE ROOSEVELT DAM, MARCH 18, 1911.

United States National Archives

mad, he escaped while being transported to the territorial prison in Yuma.

"Make sure the Kid don't catch you," the ranchers would say when we left, like that was a standard way of saying goodbye in those parts. Sightings of the Apache Kid kept coming until the early '20s, although no one knows if any of them were true because no one ever did catch the Kid.

Still, just thinking about the Apache Kid, Wyatt Earp, and the Clantons made me excited. So when we pulled into Globe,

I asked Mr. Westgard to take some photographs—the only time I asked him to do such a thing—even though the sight of the new four-storey courthouse and jail with its gallows out back made me a little uneasy. Why would a town this small need a four-storey jail and a permanent lynching spot? Maybe this still was the Wild West.

Two days after leaving Globe, we reached the shores of one of the largest lakes I had ever seen. It stretched for miles in every direction, fading into the horizon, so you couldn't tell where it ended. The lake was surrounded by desert—the White Mountains and foothills of Apache country now well behind us—and I couldn't fathom how it got there. How did this much water manage to collect on land so arid it burned the palm of your hand when you touched it?

We drove toward the giant lake while passing saguaro cacti, spoonplants, beargrass, and chollas. Not even the plants gave me a clue as to what that lake was doing in front of us. If the valley could support a lake like this, why were there no junipers or willows or wildflowers, the sort of things you would expect to see growing beside water?

The lake was so large, we spent most of the day approaching it, the water soon filling the horizon. Miles and miles of water. Only when we were nearly there did I finally spy a river running to the north of the lake. I tracked the river to the shore of the lake and noticed for the first time a concrete structure at the confluence. Mr. Westgard already had his spyglasses out, trained on the spot.

"So they have finally done it," I heard him mutter under his breath. "My Lord, they have finally done it."

I stopped driving so I could use the glasses as well. I put them to my eyes and adjusted the focus. Suddenly, a structure appeared in the prisms and mirrors of the spyglasses that startled me so much I nearly dropped them. I

stared for several minutes, not believing what I was looking at.

When I put the glasses down, I passed them to Mr. Thompson, saying: "You're not going to believe this."

"The Roosevelt Dam," said Mr. Westgard as both Mr. Thompson and I stared at the masonry wall in front of us. "I am told it is the largest dam of its kind in the world."

Mr. Westgard told us how he had watched the dam being built for the last six years, hundreds of workers camped beside the confluence of the Toto and Salt rivers in a makeshift camp larger than most towns in the territories.

"This is what can happen, gentlemen, when the federal government gets involved. A lesson for the Good Roads Movement, I would think."

The dam, with irregular blocks of stone soaring to the sky, reminded me of photos I had seen of pyramids in Egypt. There were parapets on top of the dam and a spill-water gate letting water through when we arrived so that it partially looked like Niagara Falls as well. Majestic. Everything about the structure was majestic.

I estimated the height to be more than 300 feet, the width perhaps three times that. A brick mountain built right into a river gorge. Mr. Westgard kept talking while Mr. Thompson and I stared in wonder at the dam. He told us how, in 1902, the Federal Reclamation Act was passed, which gave the federal government the authority to take over private irrigation projects it considered to be in the national interest.

Until then, irrigation projects were private affairs, sometimes started by a company, sometimes by local municipalities, that raised the money and went out to hire architects and workers. Many of the projects never got off the ground. Others got half built, and then the people building them ran out of money. The United States was littered with half-finished dams.

This dam cost 10 million dollars, and it was hard for me to imagine anyone other than the United States government being able to build it. Who would have that much money? Who would have that much tenacity? For surely this was not an easy task, something Mr. Westgard confirmed when he said that, in the first year of construction, the dam was flooded away not once, but twice.

After we finished staring at the dam, we got back into the truck and drove to the lake behind it—more properly a reservoir—which had flooded the Sonoran Desert. More than one hundred miles of shoreline. Nearly 200 feet in depth. Water backed up pretty near all the way to Utah.

"A garden from the desert," I heard Mr. Westgard say when we parked the truck. "This will change everything."

When we reached Phoenix, we were told the Roosevelt Dam had officially opened on March 18, with former president Theodore Roosevelt there to throw the switch. We had missed him by less than a month.

Carl Fisher and
the Indianapolis Speedway

The day after we arrived in Phoenix, Governor Richard Sloan, a tall, hawk-nosed former judge, came to call on Mr. Westgard. The two men shook hands warmly in the lobby of the hotel, or at least as warmly as a judge can muster, which was two shakes of the hand instead of one. He came calling with the president of the local chamber of commerce and the vice-president of the Southern Good Roads Committee. "Mr. Westgard," said the governor, "I trust your drive here was uneventful."

"It is never uneventful reaching Phoenix, Governor," said Mr. Westgard. "The passage over the White Mountains was the most grueling of any journey I have made over that mountain range to date."

"Ah, well, there is much work to be done in the mountains, I grant you. But what of the roads here in town? Have you seen our electric streetcar yet?"

Mr. Westgard said he had not seen the streetcar but had certainly heard it. It had kept him up most of the night. I tell you, there was

no pleasing the man sometimes. Still, the governor seemed to take no offense nor did the other men. When Mr. Thompson came down from his room, the five of them went into the dining room of the hotel for a lengthy breakfast. Left to my own devices, I purchased a copy of the *Arizona Republican* from the hotel newsstand and went to my room to read.

There was a story on the front page about an airplane going non-stop from London to Paris. A Frenchman named Pierre Prier was the pilot, and there were paying passengers on the flight. I read the story in wonder, not able to make up my mind who had been the bravest—the pilot or the passengers.

I flipped to the sports pages and read a lengthy story about Walter Johnson—the "Big Train"—pitching four strikeouts in a single inning for the Washington Senators, a story that confused me until I re-read it and understood that the catcher for the Senators had not fielded the ball cleanly on one of the strikeouts, allowing the batter to get on base.

There was another story about automaker

Hugh Chalmers, suggesting the American Baseball League give an annual trophy to the league's "most valuable player." That seemed like a good idea to me, and if I were given a vote, Johnson would certainly be my man. At the very bottom of the page was a small story about an auto race to be held in Indianapolis the next month on Decoration Day. It was going to be a 500-mile race on an oval track at a place called the Indianapolis Speedway.

The story quoted a man named Carl G. Fisher saying he hoped for better success than the first running of the race, which I gather had been some sort of disaster. The story ended with him talking about a national coast-to-coast road being needed in the United States, and that cars were the future of America.

I showed the story to Mr. Westgard and Mr. Thompson after their breakfast with the governor, and Mr. Westgard said he had met Carl Fisher once.

"He is a fervent believer in the Good Roads Movement," said Mr. Westgard. "A man of vision and tremendous energy, the sort of man the movement needs. Even though I have doubts about this Indianapolis Speedway notion, given what happened two years ago."

We had many things to do that day—re-provisioning the truck, sending off telegrams, looking to see if there was a Mormon church in Phoenix—so I never had the chance to ask

Mr. Westgard what he meant by "given what happened two years ago."

Years later, when flipping through the Britannicas, I came upon Fisher's name and started reading. For a long time, I had trouble believing the words in front of me, couldn't understand why I had never heard of the man.

His full name was Carl Graham Fisher, and he was like P.T. Barnum or something, only instead of promoting circuses and museums, he promoted highways and auto racing. He not only started the Indianapolis Motor Speedway, he built the first transcontinental highway in the United States.

He was born in Greensburg, Indiana, his father a drunkard who left the family when Fisher was a child. As if that weren't enough of an obstacle, the man was also born with astigmatism, an eye disorder that can cause migraine headaches and blurred vision. There are treatments for that sort of thing, but because Fisher was poor, he wasn't able to do anything about it.

He dropped out of school at the age of twelve to help support his family, working in grocery stores and bookstores, but I gather he was never happy working for another man because he was soon hawking tobacco and newspapers to people waiting at the Indianapolis train station. He'd buy his wares at a dry goods store not far from the station then mark everything up by a penny.

CARL FISHER IN 1904 AT THE HARLEM RACE TRACK IN HARLEM, ILLINOIS.

Chicago History Museum

In 1891, he opened a bicycle repair shop with two of his brothers. I had to wonder if his bad eyes steered him toward promotional work because you sort of had to figure anyone with astigmatism would make a lousy repairman. So instead of working in the shop, Fisher spent his days dreaming up new ways to bring in customers.

I had to laugh at some of the things he did. For instance, he started holding bicycle races around Indianapolis, really tough races that were hard on both the riders and the bikes. By a strange coincidence, the front of the Fisher brothers' bike repair shop was always the finish line.

Another time, when the Fishers started selling bicycles, he dropped a bike off the tallest building in Indianapolis to show people how tough it was. The Indianapolis police arrested him for that stunt, but if he sold even one more bike, I bet you the man would have thought it was worth a night in jail.

It wasn't long before the bicycle shop started selling horseless carriages as well. By this time, Fisher could afford the corrective eyeglasses sold back then for astigmatism, and he started racing the new vehicles. Around the same time, he went into business with Barney Oldfield, one of the most famous car racers in the United States, the two men opening the Fisher Automobile Company, which some people will tell you was the first car dealership in the United States.

He was always looking for ways to promote his cars. Hated advertising in the back pages of the local newspapers because that's what everyone else did. Once, he attached a Stoddard-Dayton to a hot air balloon and flew the car over Indianapolis. That got him on the front page sure enough.

It wasn't long before his car dealership made him a rich man. As did his patent on Prest-O-Lite, the acetylene headlight that was part of nearly every car manufactured in America in those days. He and another business partner sold the Prest-O-Lite patent to Union Carbide in 1913 for 9 million dollars. I read the number and couldn't fathom it.

But being a millionaire only made Carl Fisher go faster, didn't slow him down one lick. He raced his cars on gravel tracks in Chicago and New York but soon complained to his friends and business partners that this was too far to go and that there should be a decent track somewhere in Indianapolis. So in 1908, Fisher and some friends purchased land on the outskirts of Indianapolis. The next year, they opened the Indianapolis Motor Speedway.

The word speedway was Fisher's idea and it seemed to sum up the man perfectly. Speed is the way. Never slow down. Never admit defeat. Even when everything in the world is stacked up against you. Just go faster.

The opening of the Indianapolis Motor Speedway, like Mr. Westgard hinted, was a disaster. The motorcycle races that August weekend went relatively well, but the automobile races afterward were nothing less than carnage. Five people were killed. The gravel track just couldn't handle the speed of the cars, throwing rocks into the face of the drivers and spectators, leading to spin out after spin out.

His friends and business partners were beside themselves, wondering what they had done, feeling guilty about it, already looking for different ways to use the land—or selling it outright—when Fisher shocked them by saying they should try again. Their problem, he said, was simple: they needed to get rid of the gravel. It clearly didn't work on a speedway. They needed to find a new surface for the track. Fisher suggested bricks.

"But, Carl," one of his friends asked, "how many bricks do you think that would take?"

"I have no idea," he said. "Let's go find out."

The answer turned out to be 3.2 million. The work took nearly a year but by May 30, 1910 (Decoration Day Weekend), Fisher reopened the Indianapolis Motor Speedway. The next year, they extended the length of the Decoration Day Race to 500 miles, and more than 80,000 people came out to watch. Although it didn't officially become the Indianapolis 500 until some years later, that weekend was the first running of what would soon become one of the world's most famous automobile races.

Carl Fisher had so much energy, so many crazy ideas, I couldn't stop reading about him. Becoming rich with the first auto dealership in America would have been enough for most men. So would building the Indianapolis Motor Speedway. But Fisher was just getting started.

Soon after the first Indianapolis 500, he held a dinner party for some of his friends and business associates, a dinner where he announced it was time to build a "rock highway" across the United States, and what's more, his dinner guests should pay for it.

"Let's do this now," he told all those fancy people, "so we may be around to enjoy it."

His friends pledged one million dollars that night. The next year, he helped found the Lincoln Highway Association. (I gathered from reading the Britannicas that the writer had to say "helped found" because another man was chosen to lead the association even though it looked like a one-man Fisher crusade to me.)

Most of the Lincoln Highway was already there, what with frontier trails and some of the early motor paths. Mr. Westgard had mapped parts of the future highway for the American Automobile Association. It was Fisher's idea, though, to connect everything into one continuous road.

He said it would cost 10 million dollars to build the highway, so he didn't stop looking for money after his dinner party. Kept knocking on doors even though a lot of them got slammed in his face. Henry Ford hated the idea of businessmen paying to build roads. Said that was the job of the government. Refused to give the Lincoln Highway Association so much as a dime in spite of the fact he owned one of the largest car companies in the States at the time.

Lots of other people gave Fisher money, though. Theodore Roosevelt sent him a cheque. So did Thomas Edison. The reason we know this is because Fisher told newspaper reporters about every donation. When Woodrow Wilson sent a five-dollar cheque, Fisher issued the president a "highway licence" and made sure the press knew about that as well.

The fund-raising effort worked. On October 31, 1913 — even though large sections of the highway were yet to be macadamized or even cut — the Lincoln Highway was opened. That was the first coast-to-coast highway in the United States. Right after that, he built the Dixie Highway, which stretched from the Canadian border in Michigan all the way to south Florida. Again he asked for donations. Again he used the frontier trails and paths that were already there to cobble together a national road.

He also made sure the highway ran through his home state of Indiana and, years later, told a reporter he came up with the idea of the Dixie Highway so people in Indiana would have an easy way to vacation in Florida. Carl Fisher had gumption. Enough to take your breath away.

The Britannicas went on with more stories about Fisher—how he built Miami Beach from nothing but a half-finished wooden bridge and a mango-covered island; how he put up the first electric billboard in Times Square; how he once got a circus elephant to caddy for president-elect Warren Harding. But it seemed like his car and highway phase ended with the Dixie Highway.

I did read that in 1925 Fisher was one of the richest men in America, worth more than 100 million dollars. He lost everything in the stock market crash of 1929.

Love of Work

In the three days we were in Phoenix, the temperature started to go crazy, reaching heights I had never experienced before. Although it was only late April—the time of year when ice would have been gone off the rivers and lakes around Campbell's Bay for less than a month—the mid-morning temperature in Phoenix was more than one-hundred-degrees Fahrenheit.

We left town shortly before midnight with the aim of getting as far across the Sonoran Desert in the dark as we could manage. Mr. Westgard had plotted a course that would get us to the safety of a mining camp or a railway siding by early afternoon of each day, so we could avoid travelling during the hottest part of the days. Before leaving the garage, I gave the Pioneer Freighter a thorough inspection to make sure it was ready for what lay ahead.

The truck had held up remarkably well going through rivers, mud-fields, arroyos, volcanic valleys, torrential rains, sand storms, bitterly cold days and nights. Now it was to be given one more test—let's see how well you do driving through the guts of a steam-room boiler. If the Pioneer Freighter could pull this off, then maybe trucks really were work vehicles to rival trains. Maybe they really were proper tools for a working man.

I had worked with bad tools before, and they weren't just an annoyance. It was more than that. Like when a wooden sweep broke on a timber crib because someone had made the middle of the shaft too thin or chosen the wrong kind of wood out of laziness more than anything because there was plenty of ironwood around if you knew where to look for it and were willing to make the trek.

So, sure, things like that were annoying. Made you cuss a little. It was even dangerous because the sweep no doubt broke when you were straining to keep the crib under control going through some white water or fighting your way out of an eddy.

But it was more than that. Shoddy work was an insult. That's the part that always got to me. To be working hard, trying to do your best job, and then someone trips you up because they were lazy or indifferent or didn't understand the importance of work, how it was probably the most important force in the world outside of gravity—it was insulting to be at the mercy of people like that.

I know a lot of people will disagree with me, but I believe it's true. You can say love is a more powerful force than work, but think it through and tell me I'm wrong. Ask a man what he's doing, and he'll never tell you I'm falling in love. Most days he'll tell you, I'm working. Or I worked today. Or I'm trying to make it work. It's like breathing. The sort of thing that fills your days and keeps you moving; gives meaning to all this crazy stuff around you.

There's a beauty to work. Watch a finishing carpenter late in the day. See how his eye lines up the grain of the wood, looking for the right line, his blood singing. For my money, it's more inspiring than a Sunday morning choir.

Maybe I'm wrong to discount love or religion in this sort of way. Maybe it's a combination of things—love of work or something like that. But a man who doesn't respect work, who spends his life trying to avoid it or skirt it, I have no time for a man like that. Even though I feel sorry for him for throwing away his life.

So I was mighty impressed with the Pioneer Freighter and I was looking forward to seeing how she would do on the run through the desert. Seeing how she would work.

The Sonoran Desert
and a Lost Prospector

On our second day through the desert, we came upon a man wandering near the road. We spied an image of something in the distance as the sun came up behind us and lit the road ahead, none of us certain at first what we were seeing. As we got closer, we saw it was a man dressed like a prospector—denim pants, canvas shirt, full beard—yet he carried no equipment. Nor was there a horse or mule anywhere in the vicinity that we could see.

I drove the truck off the road and approached him. The man stumbled like a drunkard; his lips were cracked and caked with puss, his eyes half-closed as though he had lost the ability to open them fully. When I parked the truck, he lurched his way toward us.

"Have you seen it?" he asked.

None of us answered, not even Mr. Westgard who was never at a loss for words. The man repeated his question:

"Have you seen it?"

"Seen what?" asked Mr. Thompson.

"The way. It was here yesterday. I was almost there."

Again, we didn't know how to answer. We all craned our necks and looked around, searching for the companion, the animal, the mine entrance that would explain why this man was out here. Finally, Mr. Westgard spoke:

"You're a prospector, right, sir?"

"A prospector, yes, that be right. Have you seen the way?"

"You're in need of water. You are hallucinating. Come to the truck so we can give you some water."

The man made no movement toward the truck, just weaved back and forth on his feet, occasionally wiping long hair away from his face. Mr. Westgard got out of the truck, walked to the man and gently led him toward us. Mr. Thompson was already opening his canteen, thrusting it toward the man, then lifting it and pouring the water into the man's mouth when he made no attempt to grab it.

After a few seconds of cold water splaying over his lips, the man opened his eyes a notch and took the canteen. We all stood back as he drained the water into his mouth, coughing loudly when the canteen was empty, a horrible retching cough that buckled his knees and brought him crashing to the ground. Mr. Thompson and I jumped out of the truck.

"Water," he mumbled. "More water."

Mr. Thompson ran to get another canteen while I sat the man up. When he had the second canteen in his hands, he drained that one as well, once again coughing when he finished although not as badly this time.

"Where are you going?" Mr. Thompson asked. "Is there a mining camp around here somewhere? There's nothing marked on our maps."

The man took a badly sun-burned hand and wiped it across his lips. Then he looked up at Mr. Thompson.

"So you don't know the way."

"The way to what?"

"If you don't know then I'm not telling you. What kind of fool do you take me for?"

"Sir, you're not making any sense. Do you have a companion nearby? Is there someone travelling with you?"

"The last man was a thief," said the man, now struggling to his feet. "Don't travel with anyone no more. Won't be stole from again."

None of us knew what to say so we stood in silence as the man stood up straight and brushed some more hair away from his face. According to our map, we were forty miles from the nearest mining camp and more than sixty from the nearest rail line. It made no sense, this man being here.

"So none of you know the way."

"I'm afraid we don't," said Mr. Westgard. "Would you like to accompany us to the next camp? Perhaps someone there will know the way."

The man broke into a lecherous smile.

"You'd like that, wouldn't you? Follow me right to my claim, I bet. No one's going to steal from me again. Not you and certainly not those boys you brought with you."

"Very well. Might I offer you some water then to take for your journey?"

The man stared at Mr. Westgard with suspicion bordering on hatred, but when a canteen was placed in his hands, he snapped it to his chest in a hurry. Then he snarled:

"What are you waiting for? Get on your way."

Mr. Thompson, who was bewildered by what was happening, had to be almost dragged back to the Pioneer Freighter. I had seen this once or twice, though, in the spring when a trapper stumbled into Campbell's Bay after a winter in the bush, and I gathered from Mr. Westgard's actions that he had seen it before, too.

"We can't just leave him out here," said Mr. Thompson angrily. "He will surely die."

"He should have died already," said Mr. Westgard. "He's in God's hands now. Unless you want your throat slit in the middle of the

CURIOUS BYSTANDERS WATCH THE PIONEER FREIGHTER DRIVE BY.

night, I suggest we do as the man requests."

We drove away. The man stood rock still behind us, not turning his head, making sure we were given no clues as to "the way." Dreams gone wrong are some of the hardest things in life to witness.

I soon realized that, when taking a road trip through the desert, the land had both good and bad going for it. There were plenty of irrigation ditches, which had been a problem for us up until then, but most of the bridges over the ditches were well built and could support the weight of the truck. The land was arid and dangerous, but it was also flat and firm, the truck having no trouble going into fourth gear for long stretches. Except for the heat, it was the easiest part of the trip so far.

The heat was something else, though. They called this stretch of road the Valley of the Sun, and I had no trouble understanding why. There wasn't even a cloud in the sky, just a high cirrus white line, like some sort of frame around a painting of nothing but robin egg's blue. It was easy to follow the trail we were on, and even without stone markers, it would have been easy. We were following the sun as it tracked across the sky, as straight west as a compass arrow would have taken us.

It was still mining country for the most part, but there were no camps of any size. The mines out here were small affairs, the men going after quartz, turquoise, amethyst, and other gems. You saw the wooden frames showing the opening of the mine but never saw a miner. They were underground, digging for gems, no doubt glad to be under the Valley of the Sun.

The biggest town we reached on that stretch was called Quartzville, and after the miners came up from underneath the ground, they joined us around our cook fire, showing us the rocks they foraged for, large quartz crystals imbedded in granite. We sat around the cook fire and held the rocks, the flames turning the quartz strange colours as if you were watching hardwood leaves changing right in your hands. You imagined them being hot although they were cool to the touch and beautiful to look at.

The next morning we left early and, within an hour, were standing beside the bank of the Colorado River, staring at the far shore and the state of California.

Tricking a Ferry Operator
on the Colorado River

We had a problem.

Mr. Westgard had decided not to try to cross the Colorado River at Yuma or at Needles because there were no bridges and he worried about the weight of the truck on the ferries that ran from those towns. So we arrived at Ehrenberg instead, where a large metal barge had been in operation the year before.

But, as soon as we arrived, we were told that the barge had been lost during the spring floods. The barge that was left to keep the ferry crossing open looked like a wooden fishing skiff, and the man who owned it said there was no way it would support the weight of the truck. He was sorry, but we had to turn back.

I think we would have started living in Ehrenberg rather than turn back. Mr. Thompson and I looked at each other in disbelief. There seemed to be no way to continue the journey. Just then, Mr. Westgard started talking to the ferry operator, telling the man he was right. Of course he was right. There was no way the fully loaded truck could make its way across the Colorado River on his barge.

But what, wise sir, if the truck were unloaded of its cargo? Perhaps the barge would support its weight then?

The ferry operator was a gnome-like man with a belly sticking over his belt. He appeared to be as wide as he was tall. After thinking about it some, he agreed that might be possible, so we started hauling out the camping equipment: the barrels of gasoline, oil, and water, the oak planks. We loaded his barge with all our gear, and his Indian workers poled it across the Colorado River.

When we were back on the Arizona side, the ferry operator looked at the truck and shook his head. It was still too heavy for his little wooden skiff. And Mr. Westgard said the man was absolutely right; he had been thinking the exact same thing. My goodness, but he was a skilled and knowledgeable ferry operator.

But what if the truck were stripped to its frame? What if we removed the canvas tarps, the Ocean-to-Ocean sign, the mechanical parts—what if we took off the hood, for heaven's sake—perhaps the truck could get across then?

The ferry operator thought about it some more, scratched his belly, and said that might be possible. So we set about stripping the Pioneer Freighter, removing the tarps and the wooden bed, the carburetor, the magneto ignition, the battery, the hood. We loaded everything except the frame and the motor into the barge and poled it across the river. By now we had been working most of the day.

When we returned to the Arizona shore, the ferry operator was still dubious. He had already lost one barge that spring. He didn't want to run the risk of losing another. Mr. Westgard said he understood perfectly. How could any businessman, even one as obviously skilled and hard-working as our gnome-like friend, sustain the loss of two barges in a single season?

And if such a thing were to happen, would anyone come to his aid? Would the government assist him? Would the local chamber of commerce? In this world, hard-working men have only their wits and their brawn to protect them. Such has always been the case since the first pages of the almighty, Holy Bible.

The ferry operator scratched his belly and said Mr. Westgard was a pretty smart man, himself. To which Mr. Westgard responded by telling the ferry operator it was for this reason—the well being and future prosperity of the hard-working ferry operator—that he felt compelled to point out the somewhat obvious:

"Most of our truck is now on the other side of the river. I am afraid we will be tying up your barge for another day, just to bring everything back to Arizona."

There were already two travellers on horseback behind us waiting to board the barge, and when they heard Mr. Westgard talking, they looked at each other in confusion. Was the barge really going to be out of commission for another day? Maybe they should leave and come back later. Or start heading to Yuma. The ferry operator seemed to catch the cowboys' confused looks out of the corner of his eye and scratched his belly a little faster.

"I certainly would not wish that to happen," continued Mr. Westgard, "especially when I can guarantee you the truck is now light enough to be transported on your fine wooden barge."

"You can guarantee a thing like that?"

"Why, certainly. Let us shake on it."

Mr. Westgard stuck out his hand. The ferry operator hesitated for a second but then stuck out his hand as well.

With the deal accomplished, and even though the day was late and the sun well on its downward arc, we pushed the truck onto the wooden barge, the Indians smiling and helping us as if they were working for us instead of their regular boss. Almost immediately, the boat sank to the gunnels, causing a look of panic to run across the face of the ferry operator.

"Hold it," he said quickly, "maybe we should talk about this for a minute."

"Have no fear," said Mr. Westgard, "if it sinks no further, we shall be fine."

Which is sort of like saying, "If I don't die tonight, I'll be alive in the morning," although it confused the ferry operator long enough for the Indians to start poling the ferry away from shore. Mr. Westgard told the men to pole as fast as they could. The attempt was on. There was no turning back now even though the ferry operator started yelling something to Mr. Westgard about being tricked, and he better damn well have money in his pockets when he was fished out of the river.

We left him there, turning red in the face as we travelled a mile down river looking for a safe spot to cross, none of us wanting to be out on the river if a strong current took us. Even then, there were some hairy moments in the middle channel when water began lapping over the edge of the barge, and the Indians had a hard time keeping it straight against the wind.

When we finally reached the shores of California, everyone let out a loud whoop of celebration. There were pats on the back all way round. Mr. Thompson did a little jig he was so happy.

Because we were no longer at the regular ferry crossing, the Indians jumped ashore and started cutting a path through the tall reeds and brambles that ran beside the Colorado River, clearing a path back to the road. We pushed the truck off the barge, and I started putting her back together.

When the Indians came back, we thanked them for the fine job they had done, and Mr. Thompson put a gold coin in each of their hands, which delighted them greatly. When they left, we set up our tent and stayed right where we were for the night, figuring it best to return to the road first thing the following morning so we wouldn't have to spend the night listening to the ferry operator cussing us out from across the river.

Indian Slough

The next morning, we were all in a good mood, particularly Mr. Westgard, who had done a wonderful job getting us across the Colorado River.

"California, gentlemen," he said cheerfully, "I think it is time to see what sort of headway the Pioneer Freighter can make to Los Angeles."

I cooked us a fine breakfast of pork sides and dark beans, sliced the last of the pear-shaped tomatoes a Spanish farmer had sold to us outside Quartzville. I made a strong pot of coffee, and we sat by the cook fire longer than usual, looking at the Colorado River and laughing some more at how we managed to cross it.

Then we climbed into the truck and made our way back to the road. Fifteen minutes later, the smiles vanished from our faces as we stared at an obstacle that looked like it was going to end our journey right there.

Indian Slough. I'll never forget it.

The flooding on the Colorado River had been so exceptionally strong that year—sweeping away barges and livestock for hundreds of miles along her banks—it also created temporary lakes up and down the California shoreline.

The lakes were formed from water trapped in valleys and ravines when the river receded. In front of us was a lake—a slough is the proper name—that looked big enough to stock lake trout. It stretched for miles in every direction. We couldn't see where it ended. I waded into the water to see how deep it was but quickly realized depth didn't matter. The bottom of the temporary lake was a mire of mud and ooze. The truck would get trapped long before water depth was an issue.

I think this was the lowest point of the trip for all of us. To have come so far, to have put so much work into getting the truck across the United States, over mountains, across deserts, past arroyos, canyons, switchbacks, to have travelled across stretches of land so desolate and lonely it looked like the land God gave to Cain. To have done all that, and now the only direction left to travel was reverse.

None of it seemed fair. None of it seemed

just. The world had just turned cruel and mocking. The lowest point of the road trip, and there didn't seem to be a thing we could do about it.

Just then, Mr. Westgard started unbuttoning his military-style frock coat. Mr. Thompson and I looked at him in surprise as he stripped to his undergarments then used his belt to tie everything together into a parcel he placed upon his head. After that, he started wading into the black pool of ooze and mud, and for a moment, I thought he had turned suicidal. He had invested too much time and energy in this trip, and now that it was a failure, he was going to end his days at the spot where he had driven his last mile. But instead of collapsing in defeat, he kept wading further and further into the slough, yelling over his shoulder as he began to swim:

"I shall be back in a few hours. Good luck with the mosquitoes, gentlemen!"

We heard the entire story later. How Mr. Westgard had come through Ehrenberg the year before and knew that on the other side of the Colorado River, though not marked on any map, was a small town named Blythe. It had sprung up almost overnight because of a private irrigation system financed by some businessmen from San Francisco, who had purchased land along the river.

Mr. Westgard swam across the slough, got dressed, and walked into the irrigation town.

As it was a Sunday, he found several men eating lunch at a local diner. In the diner was the man in charge of the irrigation project, who also happened to be president of the local chamber of commerce.

"It is a pleasure to meet you, sir," said Mr. Westgard. "My name is A.L. Westgard, and I have the wonderful pleasure of travelling through your fine town today."

The man, who looked like an old cowhand, picked up a napkin, patted his lips, then placed the napkin down carefully and accepted the hand dangling in front of his face.

"It's a pleasure to meet you as well, Mr. Westgard. Just travelling through, you say?"

"That is correct, sir. Just passing through. Although it is a special journey, decidedly, that brings me your way."

"Special? How come?"

"Well, we are travelling in a Saurer Motor Company truck, sir. The latest advancement in the horseless carriage. Have you heard of it before?"

"A Saurer truck?"

"Yes, sir, a Saurer truck."

"No, can't say that I have. Although we get a few horseless carriages here from time to time."

"Yes, well, our truck is much like a horseless carriage although it is designed to carry cargo. To be a workhorse, if you will."

The man thought about that for a moment.

CROSSING INDIAN SLOUGH AFTER A FLOOD ALONG THE COLORADO RIVER.

Finally he said:

"Like a mule?"

"Well, you could say that."

"A mule," he said reflectively.

"Well, its true rival would probably be the train. Perhaps it would be best to look at it that way. As a competitor for the train."

"Not like a mule anymore?"

"No, like a train."

The head of the chamber of commerce nodded his head and took a cigar from his vest pocket.

"So what makes your trip on this not-a-mule thing so special?"

"Well, we are travelling on our truck from coast to coast across the entire breadth of these glorious states of ours. A grand adventure we are on."

At this, the man stopped lighting his cigar and peered at Mr. Westgard through the blue haze.

"Across the entire continent? That's your journey?"

"Indeed it is. Which has brought me to your fair town where, I must admit, we have encountered a problem."

"The slough."

"That is correct, sir. Although I believe I

have a remedy for the problem if I can convince you and a few of your more enterprising citizens—brawny men such as yourself, I am hoping—to assist me."

"Why do they have to be enterprising?" asked the man now happily smoking a well-lit cigar but looking at Mr. Westgard with suspicion. Perhaps the stranger was selling something.

"Because it is somewhat of a business proposal what I wish to discuss with you. Your town, young though it may be, may benefit greatly from what I am about to suggest."

The man sighed but finally stood up from his table, hitched his pants, and said:

"All right, why don't you show me this not-a-mule thing that brought you into town. We can talk along the way."

Mr. Westgard and the men from the Blythe Chamber of Commerce marched their way back to Indian Slough, bringing horses and mules with them. As they travelled, Mr. Westgard explained he was mapping a route to California, a route that would one day be taken by thousands of automobiles and trucks that were soon to follow.

The route could pass through Yuma. The route could pass through Needles. He was partial, though, to a route that would pass through Blythe, and would be even more partial to such a route, if he could find a way of fording Indian Slough.

"You can't ford it," said one of the men from the Blythe Chamber of Commerce. "Bottom is too muddy. You'll have to wait till it dries out."

"Yes, well, I believe it can be done. If you men know how to place a few dead men in the water."

The man looked at Mr. Westgard with renewed interest.

"Sounds like you know what you're talking about, Mr. Westgard. But even with the dead men, I don't know if our mules and horses will be enough."

"Well, sir, our little truck has a bit of power of her own."

When they reached the slough, Mr. Westgard swam back and told us what was happening. The men from the chamber of commerce would set up a series of dead men—timber posts placed in the water—that would be used to winch the truck across the slough. There would have to be several dead men set at a zigzagging course to keep the truck afloat. A straight line would simply break. They would have to use block and tackle as well. As much as we had. Come, gentlemen, there was work to be done.

For the next several hours, we set up the course. Then, when the work was done, I climbed behind the wheel and started the truck. Mr. Westgard stood on shore taking photos.

Like I said, Mr. Westgard could amaze

**THE BLYTHE, CALIFORNIA, CHAMBER OF COMMERCE
HELPING GET THE TRUCK ACROSS THE SLOUGH.**

you from time to time. It took us the rest of the afternoon, and I think if we were missing even one man or one mule, we never would have made it. But as the sun was sinking in front of us, I drove the truck out of the water and onto firm ground.

There was a loud cheer from the Blythe Chamber of Commerce, and we cheered along with them although I was probably the first one to stop. The truck was filthy and stank of rotten vegetation. It would take hours to clean, and sure enough, that task became mine as everyone else marched back to Blythe to continue the celebrations.

Love of work. Some days it was easier than others.

America on the Move

The next morning, we continued on our way to Los Angeles. By mid-morning, we were driving on a fine macadamized road, and by mid-afternoon, there were cars passing us fairly regularly, heading for ferry crossings across the Colorado River.

It never became the traffic block Mr. Westgard had complained about in Albuquerque, but I was still astonished at how many cars and motorcycles were now sharing the road with us. In large cities like Toronto and New York, I had become accustomed to seeing automobiles on the streets. There were even a fair number of motorized trucks—furniture vans, brewery vans, newspaper and dairy vans—all travelling down what were, in many cases, fine, paved streets.

That made sense to me. People had to go places in a city. People had to work. But out here on a road, miles from any city or factory, I couldn't explain why there were suddenly so many cars and trucks.

Mr. Westgard wasn't surprised. He said America was a country that loved to go places—*was* going places—and he told me many stories to prove this assertion: How one year he had driven the Premier Pathfinder to the Grand Canyon, one of the first men to drive a motorized vehicle to that natural wonder of the world—"a pity we will not be seeing it on this journey"—and how, when he arrived, there was only a livery to house his car for the night. The owner of the livery had to be convinced to let him use it. The next morning, Mr. Westgard told the man he should consider building a proper garage to accommodate the motorists that would soon be coming. The man laughed right in Mr. Westgard's face, told him only fools would ever make the trip, and why should he spend money building a garage for fools? Two years later, when Mr. Westgard returned to the Grand Canyon, he discovered the man had indeed built a garage, and on the night he arrived, the garage was full. He still had to stay in the livery.

Or what of the many touring clubs and motoring associations in America—that was yet more proof. How, by the turn of the century, there were clubs and associations in virtually every city of any size in the United

A FINE ROAD IN CALIFORNIA.

States even though the automobile had only come to America six years earlier and was still little more than an oddity.

There were almost too many motoring associations to count, although in 1902, the most prominent among them—the Chicago Automobile Association, Automobile Club of Utica, Automobile Club of New Jersey, Long Island Automobile Club, Grand Rapids Automobile Club, Philadelphia Automobile Club, Rhode Island Automobile Club, and the Princeton Automobile Club—all banded together to form the American Automobile Association. It became the greatest motoring club of them all, an association doing fine work for the Good Roads Movement.

It was Mr. Westgard who designed the first strip maps for the American Automobile Association, those foldout maps everyone started using a few years later. He mapped the Midland Trail and the Overland Trail for what people soon called the AAA then started doing full-fledged pamphlets for the association on car camping in New England or hunting and fishing regulations in New Mexico.

While he was a field representative with the AAA, Mr. Westgard even invented the world's first RV, a natural idea for the man. America was on the move, anxious to jump behind the wheel of a car or a truck and go someplace: the Grand Canyon, the far coast, the distant mountain range—the destination didn't matter all that much because the next year there would be a new destination. America just wanted to take a road trip. But she still had to sleep. Still had to park the car somewhere at the end of the day and find a bed. So Mr. Westgard—who always had a practical bend of mind—invented a truck that came with its own bed. And kitchen. And chairs.

He called the vehicle a Skip-Along-Bungalow, and it looked a lot, from photos I saw later, like a wooden cabin perched on four rubber tires. He travelled across the United States in the Skip-Along-Bungalow often with his wife and eldest son accompanying him, the family peering out the windows of the cabin at the countryside passing them by. The vehicle was like some little cabin being swept away on floodwaters.

Mr. Westgard talked of patenting the Skip-Along-Bungalow but never got around to it. The AAA was keeping him mighty occupied in those days, so maybe that wasn't a surprise. The association was busy lobbying the federal government for funding to build proper roads across the country, and it needed maps to show where the roads should be built.

So the AAA kept sending Mr. Westgard out West or up North or down South, so he could map new trails or see whether the old frontier trails could be adapted for use by a motorized vehicle.

The AAA also needed to show the government that a lot of people wanted these roads—average working people, the millions of people who voted for politicians and made them win or lose elections—not just a handful of well-bred scions attending Princeton University (though they could be handy as well during an election).

The membership in AAA was probably all they needed to win that argument. In 1902, there were fewer than 1,000 active members in the American Automobile Association. By 1926—five years after the United States Congress passed the Federal Highway Assistance Act—the membership had increased to 800,000.

America was on the move. The number of cars and trucks we passed on our way to Los Angeles did not surprise Mr. Westgard in the slightest.

A Showdown between Barney Oldfield and Louis Chevrolet

Even the fine state of the road we were travelling on had something to do with the American Automobile Association. The road was called the Los Angeles to Phoenix Race Road, and it was the first motor trail in the United States that didn't have a name that made you think of covered wagons or Spanish conquistadors. It got its name because of an annual road race sanctioned by the AAA that first took place in 1908. Before long, people started calling it the Cactus Derby Road, but when we passed through, it still went by its proper title.

It was a newspaper, the *Arizona Republican*, that came up with the idea of holding a race between Los Angeles and Phoenix; it was trying to show people how easy it was to drive a horseless carriage from the territorial state capital out to the Pacific Ocean. It wasn't easy at all, of course, but when a newspaper sets its mind to something, it's quite remarkable how the natural world around you can change.

So the *Arizona Republican*, with help from some local motorists in Phoenix who had formed the Maricopa Auto Club, came up with the idea of holding a race across the desert. The winner would get a nice write-up in the *Arizona Republican*. The motor club would give them a silver cup.

Four cars—owned by rich men, each with a driver—entered that first race. They left Los Angeles on November 8, 1908, driving through Pomona, Ontario, Palm Springs, Indio, then across the Colorado River at Ehrenberg, before continuing on through Quartzville, Buckeye, and finally Phoenix. The exact route we were driving. The four cars were a Kissel Kar, a White Steamer, an Elmore Bulldog, and a Franklin Greyhound. It was the steamer that pulled up first to the offices of the *Arizona Republican*, the winner being F.C. Fenner and his driver "Happy" Forbes. (As a driver, myself, I wouldn't be that happy about people forgetting my first name, but what can I say? I didn't know the man.)

The duo collected their silver cup, posed for photos with the publisher of the newspaper, and had a story published the next day.

LOUIS CHEVROLET IN A BUICK RACER AT THE COBE CUP RACE, 1909.
Chicago Historical Society

The following year, ten cars entered the race, which was won by a man named Joe Nikrent, driving a Buick. Only four cars managed to cross the finish line, there being all manner of bad obstacles they encountered. One driver hit a tree. Another sunk his car in a creek. The cars that didn't make it, you never hear much about them anymore—the Dorris, the Elmore, the Pennsylvania; there was even an Italian car, the Isotta, that was the first one to die on the race course that year.

Anyway, the race started to attract all sorts of car manufacturers and race-car drivers. The city of San Diego even held its own Cactus Derby for a couple of years, trying to show the Good Roads people that their city should be the western terminus for any national highway. San Diego was still smarting from being passed over by the railway companies a few years ear-

lier, most of which had chosen Los Angeles for the end of their lines. San Diego had a good argument, too, because their drivers made better time to Phoenix in almost every race they ran. But it was like fate was against them or something because it was the Los Angeles to Phoenix race that got all the attention and that most people remember today.

In 1912, the race was won by Ralph Hamlin, driving a Franklin, and the Franklin Automobile Company made a big deal out of that victory, using it in all sorts of promotional brochures and billboards until it seemed like the Cactus Derby was about the only race in the United States. The publicity brought out even more racers and car companies. Wealthy people from Los Angeles and Phoenix started to line the route to see the cars pass by; all those fancy people mixing with politicians

BARNEY OLDFIELD AND HENRY FORD IN 1902.
automotivehistoryonline.com

and reporters and newsreel people. The race started to resemble a state fair.

Then came 1914 and the most famous race of them all. The showdown between Barney Oldfield and Louis Chevrolet.

Aside from Cannonball Baker and Ralph DePalma, there were probably no more famous auto racers in the United States back then than Barney Oldfield and Louis Chevrolet.

Chevrolet was a Swiss-born racer who lived in Montreal for a spell (not that far from my hometown) before coming to New York City in 1900. He ended up racing Buick cars and became friends with Billy Durant, who started General Motors.

Chevrolet started as a mechanic and was famous for his car designs, crazy ideas—like a front-wheel-drive racing car or an overhead-valve six-cylinder car, which almost scared you it could go so fast. He started the Chevrolet Motor Company, but he was a lousy businessman and sold out after a few years to Durant, who folded the company into General Motors. Chevrolet went back to racing.

As for Barney Oldfield, that man was so famous there was even an expression back then that you used when someone was getting too big for his britches: "Who do you think you are, Barney Oldfield?"

He was the first man to drive a car at sixty miles an hour, doing it at the Indiana State Fairgrounds in 1903. Oldfield practically taught everyone else how to race, never hitting his brakes on the turns, just sliding into them like a motorcycle racer.

He drove a Ford for the first few years, and when he won the Manufacturers' Challenge

Cup in 1902, beating Alexander Winton by a half-mile on the five-mile course, Henry Ford fell in love with the guy. That win put the Ford Motor Company on the map.

Oldfield was a real showman and a bit of a gunslinger, willing to race anytime, anywhere, against anything. He raced against airplanes. Against trains. He once did eighteen races in twenty weeks while driving for Peerless, winning sixteen of the contests. He started getting paid 4,000 dollars per appearance, loved getting all that money and attention, but it got him into trouble with the American Automobile Association for a lot of his races were not sanctioned by the AAA. The motoring association suspended him for participating in "outlaw races." In 1914, after apologizing to the AAA, Oldfield was allowed to come back.

The Los Angeles to Phoenix Road Race was one of his first AAA-sanctioned races following the suspension. Oldfield was thirty-six and desperate for a win, desperate to be back on the front page of the newspaper.

Louis Chevrolet, who had returned to racing after a four-year absence, was also desperate for a win. The two men arrived in Los Angeles in November of 1914 already hating each other.

Besides the first-place purse money of 2,750 dollars, both men badly wanted the trophy that year, which would replace the traditional silver cup. In 1914, the trophy was going to be a diamond-encrusted medal

bearing an inscription. The inscription read: "Master Driver of the Universe."

The race would be 132 miles longer than the original course, following a different, more northerly route through Needles, California. It was scheduled for three days with two overnight stops. Oldfield was driving a Stutz Bearcat. Chevrolet was driving a car of his own design, carrying the name Chevrolet.

The weather was atrocious when the twenty drivers left Los Angeles on the morning of November 10. There was rain, sleet—some news reports even said there was hail. Eight miles into the race a driver hit a ditch and nearly died.

Oldfield and Chevrolet battled for first place throughout the day, each man taking progressively greater risks to finish first. They slid through hairpin turns, plowed through mud fields, drove one-handed as they wiped sleet off their goggles.

When they reached Needles and stopped for the night, Oldfield was in first place with a time of eight hours, fifty-five minutes, and thirty-four seconds. Chevrolet was sixteen seconds behind.

The next day, both men had car problems. Oldfield went down first with a flat tire. He walked back to Needles for a spare and resumed the race.

Chevrolet was not so lucky. Just outside of Kingman, Arizona, he hit a ditch and destroyed the frame of his car. Unable to continue the race but wanting badly to beat Oldfield, he joined the team of close friend Cliff Durant (son of Billy Durant), who was also driving a Chevrolet car.

The two racing legends raced through the Arizona desert, arriving in Prescott by early evening, again only seconds apart, Oldfield still in the lead.

On the third day, the weather turned into an absolute storm. Visibility was nil. Rivers started to flood. The rain and sleet was torrential. Chevrolet's car soon got stuck in a mud field. Oldfield's got stranded in a fast-moving creek with a silt bottom.

At this stage, Oldfield's luck turned out to be better than his rival's. A farmer with a team of mules was riding beside the creek when Oldfield got stuck and quickly pulled him free. He resumed the race, having lost only minutes of time. Durant and Chevrolet were stuck for nearly three hours.

It was Oldfield who reached Phoenix first and earned the title "Master Driver of the Universe." He won the 1914 Cactus Derby with a combined time of twenty-three hours, thirty-five seconds.

The three-hour delay for the Chevrolet team robbed the spectators in Phoenix of what might have been a dramatic finish. The Chevrolet team finished three hours, twenty-five seconds behind Oldfield.

Saying Goodbye to a Pathfinder

We weren't going to win any races driving an eight-and-a-half-ton truck, but in those last few days of our trek out west, we made good time, especially when we reached the macadamized roads of the San Bernardino Valley. On that stretch of road, we averaged nearly fifteen miles per hour.

Before getting there, we drove through the far western edge of the Sonoran Desert, both Mr. Thompson and I marvelling at the countryside around us; a crazy quilt of different rock formations and vegetation, the land never staying the same for more than a mile. I had never seen anything like it.

There were hills made of nothing but boulders as if someone had stacked them there. And a strange tree that wasn't a tree but a plant that grew as high as a small balsam with leaves that looked like pine cones. A Joshua tree, Mr. Westgard called it: a name given to it by the Mormons, for it always looked as if it was holding its branches up to the heavens.

There were canyons and gorges and small mountain ranges. We'd be driving through the desert, and then in the distance, we'd spy a giant lake—the Salton Sea, I was told—which was a salt-water lake so not even that made sense. The countryside was so strange, so mixed up and confused, it was like it was drunk.

After the desert, we started driving through orchards and vineyards, suddenly surrounded by grapes, oranges, and dates. I swear, dates. Something I had never seen growing anywhere before and that I didn't even think grew in the United States. The countryside reminded me of those kaleidoscope toys you buy at a five and dime store; the ones you shake and put to your eye, and every time you gaze through, there is a different pattern to look at, different colours to see, different thoughts left running through your head.

It was like our journey was coming to some mad, skittering finish: things moving too fast, things changing every time you looked around, like the United States was moving into another gear, trying to shove everything into your face before she was done with you.

We drove through Indio, Redlands,

THE PIONEER FREIGHTER MAKING SALES CALLS IN LOS ANGELES.

Ontario, and Pomona; I started feeling giddy. Light-headed. Began laughing at the sheer craziness of everything around me.

On May 8, we reached the outskirts of Los Angeles where several cars from the Southern California Automobile Dealers' Association were waiting to escort us into the city. With car horns sounding and people singing, we drove down Sunset Boulevard, which was the official end of Mr. Westgard's Trail to Sunset, the route he had cobbled together the year

before by using the Santa Fe Trail, the Real Camino, and the Los Angeles to Phoenix Race Road.

Los Angeles was just as big as New York but nothing like it at all. Most of the buildings were wide instead of tall and almost none of them red or brown brick. Instead, the buildings were the colours of the desert: white, yellow, washed-out-corduroy; these were buildings made of limestone or even marble, a few of them looked to be. The streets were wide and lined with palm trees. There was a warm breeze hitting

ON THE STREETS OF LOS ANGELES, WITH NEW MEXICO A DISTANT MEMORY.

us right in the face, and nothing anywhere that would make you think of a cold day back east.

We drove right down Sunset Boulevard to the Pacific Ocean and posed for photographs, Mr. Westgard, Mr. Thompson, and I standing beside the Ocean-to-Ocean sign as a photographer from the motor association went to work. Then some of the association people wanted to have their photographs taken with the truck, so I walked away.

I was still a little light-headed and, as I stared at the horizon over the ocean, I had trouble making it out—just a thin blue line showing above the water, birds flying everywhere, the sun just starting to sink. It had taken us sixty-three days to travel 1,531 miles.

I remember standing on the beach that day looking out at the ocean, feeling not tired as you might suspect but powerful, elated, as if something electric were coursing through my body and making me all hopped up. I remember thinking, if we just thought it through, if we could get the dead men placed just right, we could probably cross this last obstacle as well.

I stayed in Los Angeles for two days while Mr. Westgard and Mr. Thompson visited the presidents of some of the local motoring associations, reporters from the daily newspapers and some automotive magazines, the men who held the distribution rights to Saurer trucks in southern California. When I wasn't needed to drive the truck, I walked around the city, marvelling at the buildings, the palm trees, a Chinese section I stumbled upon that had pigs hanging from spits outside the front doors of the groceries, and men wearing black pyjamas, every second one riding a bicycle.

On the third morning, Mr. Thompson and I re-loaded the Pioneer Freighter and said goodbye to Mr. Westgard. His work for the Saurer Motor Truck Company and the Office of Public Roads was finished.

"Mr. MacLean," he said as we departed, "you have done an admirable job as my driver. One day, I hope we may travel together again across these glorious states of ours."

I shook his hand, and not knowing what else to say, said I wished the same thing. I put the truck in gear and drove away. I never saw him again.

Travelling to San Francisco with a Reporter

Now it was just Mr. Thompson and me making the journey even though his father had invited a reporter from one of the automotive magazines to join us for the trip to San Francisco. The reporter sat in the bed of the truck asking a lot of questions of Mr. Thompson while I drove. Most of the questions were silly: "If macadamized roads were built in New Mexico and Arizona, what do you think the running time would be for a truck such as the Pioneer Freighter from Denver to Los Angeles?"

Which is sort of like saying: "If the truck were a plane and you could fly, what would the running time be between Denver and Los Angeles?" Still, Mr. Thompson did an admirable job of keeping a serious face and answering all the man's questions, only occasionally winking at me but otherwise playing it straight as a railway tie. The man wore driving goggles even though there was no sand or bad weather to speak of during our trip to San Francisco, and the more he prattled, the more grateful I became that all his questions were addressed to Mr. Thompson. This didn't surprise me. I had been reading automotive magazines for a couple of years now and almost never read a quote from a driver.

As the never-ending interview dragged on, I stared around, the Pacific Ocean never far away, sometimes hidden behind a forest of tall fir trees or a rocky outcrop but then reappearing with a flash of turquoise blue. It was a much brighter ocean than the Atlantic, and I couldn't figure out why that would be. You would think an ocean would be an ocean. It wasn't like a lake that might change on you because of water depth or current or some of the stuff people dump into a lake. Why should a ton of salt water ever look any different?

Still, the proof was right beside me. I found myself wishing Mr. Westgard was still here with his camera, so we could take some photographs. I mentioned this to Mr. Thompson, who said he would purchase one in San Francisco. The reporter had a camera with him, but if he took photos the way he asked questions, I wasn't hopeful about the outcome.

ANOTHER SIGN, ANOTHER SALES CALL, THIS TIME IN SAN FRANCISCO.

The road itself was a fine macadamized affair all the way to Long Beach, then gravel for a while, then dirt. We were forever going up and down some sort of hill, which slowed us down plenty although there were no arroyos or irrigation ditches to speak of, and that evened things out. We made good time for most of this stretch. About halfway through, we even passed another truck—a Ford Model T panel truck—on its way to Los Angeles with a load of teak wood. We stopped and talked to the driver, the reporter anxious to interview him, too. He asked questions about his run and was told that this was the first time the Ford truck driver was making it; that he worked for people who imported the teak from Ceylon, and they were in a hurry to get a shipment to Los Angeles.

"The train was going to take nearly a month," he explained. "It was going to sit on the railway sidings for weeks. So they told me to see if I could drive it down."

The driver enquired then about our Ocean-to-Ocean sign, and Mr. Thompson told him we had just made a cargo run from Denver. Were on our way to San Francisco then on to New York City.

"New York City?"

"That's right."

The driver left soon afterward, looking at us as if we were drunk. Just before reaching San Francisco, we stopped at a small town called San Mateo to hook up with some cars and trucks from one of the local motoring clubs. Mr. Thompson's father had arranged the escort, and we drove into San Francisco by way of the Golden Gate Bridge, which was the biggest bridge I had ever seen. We didn't bother going to the ocean that day but went straight to our hotel; Mr. Thompson told the president of the motor club that he would see him the following day. We said goodbye to the reporter at the same time. The date was May 27.

I spent the next few days in San Francisco doing the same things I had done in Los Angeles: driving Mr. Thompson to his various appointments and walking around the city when I wasn't needed. I spent an entire afternoon on Fisherman's Wharf trying to make out the fish they were unloading from the trawlers—fish I had never seen before—and staring at the port-of-call flags on the cargo ships. The flags were a mystery to me until I started talking to an old fisherman who pointed some of them out to me: China, Ceylon, Japan, British Guinea.

Another day, we drove the Pioneer Freighter up and down the streets of San Francisco for no other reason than to display a new

sign made for us by the man who owned the distribution rights for Saurer Trucks in Northern California. Mr. Thompson was downright apologetic when he told me about it.

"We have to go to a printer, George, and pick up another sign."

"What's wrong with the one we have?" I asked.

"Absolutely nothing. This is a new sign that we have to attach to the truck to go along with our Ocean-to-Ocean sign."

I didn't think we had enough canvas for such a thing, but we fiddled with it until we finally got it to work and attached the new sign right below our sign. The signs on the truck now read: "Saurer Motor Truck, Ocean-to-Ocean, Pioneer Freighter. Agents: Motor Sales of Cal., 346 Golden Gate Ave." We had to move the Goodrich Tires sign to the rear of the truck to squeeze it all in. The only thing we were now missing was the bearded lady and the monkey boy.

The man on Golden Gate Avenue had also built what he called a "display room," where people could see the cars and trucks he was selling. The room was right on the street behind plate glass, so people could see the merchandise without the bother of actually walking inside. Mr. Thompson had to spend two days in the display room, standing beside the Pioneer Freighter, handing out pamphlets to anyone who asked for one. The first day, I stayed in the display room until Mr.

THE PIONEER FREIGHTER AT THE PACIFIC OCEAN, JUST OUTSIDE SAN FRANCISCO.

Thompson told me I could leave. He sounded mighty embarrassed when he said:

"George, there's really no reason for both of us to be here."

I didn't bother arguing and went for a long walk through the city and found another Chinese neighbourhood even bigger than the one in Los Angeles. I went back the next day as well. I had a good lunch of vegetables wrapped in a pastry shell and drank dark tea that seemed stronger than the coffee I made on the road.

A Bridge in Kansas

On June 7, I loaded the Pioneer Freighter onto a Denver and Rio Grande railcar and said goodbye to Mr. Thompson. I was taking the truck back to Colorado, while he needed to stay in San Francisco another day on business. The route we would take to finish our ocean-to-ocean journey started at Pueblo, which we had passed through nearly three months earlier, and that's where Mr. Thompson would meet me in five days time.

"I wish I were going with you, George, but Father has made some appointments for me. There are some papers I need to sign."

"I could wait for you if you want the company," I said.

"No, it's best you head out first and get things organized. We'll want to leave as soon as I arrive."

I nodded my head and didn't say anything although it was strange to realize I was on my own now.

"Don't get too used to the train, George," said Mr. Thompson as I climbed aboard the passenger car. "We still have some travelling ahead of us."

I laughed at the admonishment although as I sat in the train for the next three days, it was hard not to think how much easier this was. I was somewhat taken aback by the thought because it seemed almost treasonous—after all those truck demonstrations in the mining camps, all those conversations around the cook fire about the Good Roads Movement and the future of America—so I pushed the thought away as hard as I could. Spent my days reading newspapers and automotive magazines while the Rocky Mountains drifted slowly by.

When the train reached Pueblo, I helped a couple of roustabouts unload the truck and drove it to a livery. After that, I checked into a hotel then started looking for a hired hand in need of some short-term work; Mr. Thompson had told me to hire a man to accompany us as far as Kansas City. Mr. Westgard had warned us it could be tough travelling over the Great Plains, especially if we got any rain. I didn't make the same mistake Mr. Thompson made of hiring a man in a casino but enquired at the telegram office. The man there directed me to a farm where a tall, strapping sixteen-year-old quickly got permission from his father to accompany us as long as we agreed to pay the son's train fare back to Pueblo in addition to his wages.

"I've never been to Kansas City," said the boy, whose name was Will Foster. "I hear they have electric street cars and everything."

I told him I had never been to Kansas City either, but had heard the same thing. His father told me the boy would be at the train station in two days time and made me promise to feed him well.

I next went out and purchased food, gas, and oil, all the while feeling a bit out of place about being back in Colorado with no ocean to look at, with the Rocky Mountains again to the west of me, and the Great Plains to the east. Made me feel like I was about to check into the Brown Palace Hotel for the first time and await the arrival of a gentleman named A.L. Westgard. That feeling of being taken back in time—as though I had just snapped out of a long dream and everything I'd being doing recently wasn't real—it didn't disappear for days. Only the sun rising over the Great Plains told me something was different.

Mr. Thompson arrived early in the morning of the third day and seemed mighty glad to see me.

"I have had enough of display rooms, George, I can tell you that. I felt like a monkey at a zoo."

"Did you sell any trucks?" I asked.

"I may have sold one. There was a gentleman who came back to see me three times. I'm expecting a telegram when we get to Dodge City."

Which was no. Still, Mr. Thompson was in such a good mood, I didn't bother to point this out. Told him the truck was all loaded, and the hired hand was to meet us at the train station within the hour.

"He's a farm boy," I said. "His father wants us to feed him well, pay him a dollar a day, and put him on the train back to Pueblo when we get to Kansas City."

"He doesn't claim to be the best mechanic in Pueblo, does he, George?"

"No, he doesn't say much of anything, really. Just wants to see an electric street car."

"A good choice, George. A good choice."

We went to pick up the Pioneer Freighter and then returned to the train station, where Will and his father were waiting. Mr. Thompson shook the old man's hand, promised to feed his son well, and with that, we left Pueblo at mid-morning of June 12. As it turned out, Will Foster had a pretty easy go of it for we had nothing but fine weather that week, no mud to speak of and even most of the irrigation ditches had good wooden culverts we could drive right over.

We reached La Junta, which is on the northern banks of the Arkansas River, our second night out. It was once a major trading post along the Santa Fe Trail. There was still an adobe trading fort in the middle of the small town, and a hotel owner told us trappers still used the post every spring to sell their hides.

Two days later, we entered Kansas, just past the town of Holly. We were on the Great Plains proper now, not just hugging the edge, and you could see for miles without anything blocking the horizon. The sky was the colour of faded denim, the clouds those thick, cumulus kind that made you think of cotton hanging heavy on the vine. It was such fine driving, we kept going long into the night, stopping only to spread our bedrolls, not even bothering with a cook fire.

The next day, we reached Dodge City, a place I had read plenty about when I was a boy. Will had also read some stories and was amazed when we told him Wyatt Earp was still alive and living in the San Bernardino Valley in California, which we had driven through the month before.

"Did you see Mr. Earp?" he asked and was obviously disappointed when we told him, no, we were in a hurry and had never thought to track him down. We stopped for lunch at a hotel, and Will asked at the front desk for directions to Boot Hill, but the man said it had been moved to a permanent cemetery some years ago and was nothing more than a small knoll now.

DRIVING ACROSS THE GREAT PLAINS.

We made quick time to Kingsley after that, which is roughly the halfway point of these "glorious states of ours," a fact that dawned on us only later in the day, otherwise we might have stopped to have a photograph taken with Mr. Thompson's new camera. We passed fields of sugar beets and salt mines, which was an odd mix when you stop to think about it, but most of that day we spent looking at the sky, which was as big and welcoming as the gateway to heaven, so we didn't spent much time thinking about sugar beets and salt mines.

When we reached Stafford, we found gravel roads, and then after that, macadamized roads. When we neared Hutchinson early the next day, Mr. Thompson and I had pretty much convinced ourselves the worst of our trip was over. It was a fine summer day, and we were teasing Will for having such an easy go of it: telling him how the last hired hand disappeared in the middle of the night before we even reached New Mexico. As we neared the town, farmers working in the sugar-beet fields stopped to wave at us, pointed at our Ocean-to-Ocean sign, and called over other farmers. We were all looking forward to reaching Kansas City the next day.

We drove into Hutchinson and crossed a trestle bridge over the Arkansas River. Will was thinking about electric street cars and wondering if his father expected him to catch a train right away, Mr. Thompson was thinking of the telegram he would send his father with the news of our quick time from Pueblo, and I was thinking of the bed waiting for me at the hotel in Kansas City.

Just then, with all these happy thoughts in our collective heads, the bridge collapsed.

We fell fifteen feet. Straight into the middle channel of the Arkansas River, the wooden bridge falling on top of us.

The weight of the cargo in the back of the truck pulled us in that direction, so we fell on the rear axles, the nose of the truck pointing skywards as it teetered for a minute then splashed into the river. Mr. Thompson and

Will were thrown clear of the truck and landed in the river. The steering wheel kept me inside, and if I had been knocked unconscious, I think I would have drowned that day for the water was soon over the steering wheel and within inches of the roof of the truck. Luckily, I managed to swim ashore against the strong current.

We stood there, the three of us, looking at the Arkansas River coursing around the Pioneer Freighter as if the truck were a large boulder that had always been there. The only thing visible was the roof of the canvas tarp and the top of the letters on the sign that said Saurer Pioneer Freighter, Ocean to Ocean. Or—Ocean-to-a-River-in-Kansas, which is what fate seemed to have in store for us.

The silence went on for a long time and was only broken finally by Will Foster asking: "So what do we do now?"

Much of the town of Hutchinson came out to see what had happened to its bridge. Some farmers broke into laughter when they saw us standing there on the shore as wet as a sack full of kittens. I heard one old farmer say, "See, I told you that dang silly thing wouldn't work."

I think if it had been left to the citizens of Hutchinson to decide our fate, the truck would have been left right where it landed, the Pioneer Freighter turned into some sort of navigational marker on the Arkansas River. With offers of help not forthcoming, Mr. Thompson hired a man with a team of mules to pull the truck from the river.

When the truck was back on dry land, I began my inspection. To my surprise, I saw that neither the frame of the truck nor the rear axles had been bent. Aside from some cargo that had been swept away, the truck looked pretty much the same as it had that morning.

I took out the battery and the magneto ignition and began fanning them with a canvas tarp on the banks of the river. Mr. Thompson and Will built a fire to dry what was left of our clothing and camping equipment. Our dry food was now sludge, and we threw it away.

Four hours later, I put the truck back together, turned the magneto ignition, and the engine started on the first try. Even some of the more dubious citizens of Hutchinson who felt we got what we deserved for being so foolish as to think you could drive a truck across the United States, let out a cheer. Miracles will make a fan out of anyone, I suppose. Eight hours after we had collapsed through the trestle bridge, we were ready to resume our journey.

Before we were able to leave Hutchinson, though, the county building inspector came out to look at the damage we had caused. He was a tall, thin man, dressed more like an undertaker than a civil servant, and you could tell by the way he looked at what was left of the bridge that he wasn't terribly impressed with us.

"You boys have made a fine mess of our bridge," he said as he walked toward us. The three of us stood there shuffling our feet like truant schoolboys. It was Mr. Thompson who finally spoke for us:

"Sir, I am sure that the Saurer Motor Truck Company will pay for any damages."

"I'm sure it will, too, son. Now whom do I contact to tell them what a bunch of dang fools you three have been?"

"My father."

And with that, Mr. Thompson wrote out the name of his father and an address in Chicago, gave it to the county inspector, who tipped his hat to us and then let us drive away from Hutchinson.

"I naturally asked him to remove the photos."

We reached Kansas City on June 18, travelling along the banks of the Missouri River until we reached Kaw Point where the Missouri River connects with the Kansas River. We followed the Chicago and Rock Island rail line after that to the centre of town, the line taking us past a maze of cattle pens—more livestock in one place than I had seen in my entire life. The sounds from the pens were a bit demented, so I was glad to leave them behind. There were fine paved streets once we turned away from the rail line, and we followed 16th Street until we reached the Savoy Hotel where we would stay for the next two nights.

The Savoy was a fine red-brick hotel, and after storing the Pioneer Freighter in a garage, I took advantage of the large bed in my room and had a nap. I was still somewhat rattled from the bridge collapse in Hutchinson and realized how easily we could have been killed had the truck rolled sideways when it fell, or if the current of the Arkansas River had carried us downstream.

Back home, on the Ottawa River and its tributaries, people drowned every spring. Most of the deaths came as the result of the log drives, but there were plenty of people who died because of misadventure. A child playing on the ice where he shouldn't have been. Some damn fool wading into the river to fish too early in the season. A boat that capsized simply because a gust of wind came down the Gatineau Hills when the boat was turned the wrong way.

None of those people, you had to believe, knew they were being foolish. None of them were suicidal even if everyone afterward shook their heads and wondered what in the world they were thinking when they did what they did, like it defied logic or something.

"Dang fool," someone would say when a body was brought to shore.

"Dang fool," someone else would agree.

If we had died in Hutchinson, would people have said the same thing about us? Driving a truck across the United States—was it an adventure? Or a misadventure?

I fell asleep thinking about it but I never did come up with an answer. Which was strange because the answer always seemed so obvious whenever a body was dragged from the water.

There were no saloons in Kansas City the year we were there and there may still be no saloons there, the temperance ladies having done fine work in Kansas City on both sides of the state line. It didn't bother us any although it was strange to think of a city that big without a single drinking establishment. We had just travelled through the Wild West, which seemed to have more saloons than banks. Or people for that matter.

Being in a city without saloons made me think of Mr. Westgard, whom I was surprised to discover I was missing, something I wouldn't have thought possible when I first met him.

Mr. Westgard had no patience for saloons or dance halls; he had more affinity with the temperance ladies than saloon keepers even though he enjoyed a bottle of wine with some of his hotel meals. When we were driving through Arizona, he even told us a story about once having a fight with a saloon keeper in that territory; he refused to give us the name of the town.

"The saloon was in a hotel I was staying in for the evening," he said. "Needing to speak with the owner on a matter of some import, I located him behind his bar, tending to the rather rough crowd that was gathered around him.

"As I was speaking to the gentleman, although he soon proved himself to be nothing of the sort, I noticed several photos behind his bar. The lewdest, most offensive photos I have ever seen in a public place."

He looked at us knowingly, and I tried hard not to laugh. Some of the photos I had seen being passed around on a log drive were enough to make a beaver blush. I had a good idea what sort of photos he was talking about. He nonetheless continued with his story, apparently oblivious to Mr. Thompson and me, who were biting our lips with great force.

"I naturally asked him to remove the photos immediately as they were an insult not only to his hotel and the people staying there, but to the entire town."

"Did he?" asked Mr. Thompson.

"No, he did not. As a matter of fact, he went on at great length about how it was his saloon, and he could hang whatever photographs he wished. A sentiment that was shockingly shared by the men gathered in the saloon."

Mr. Westgard said that he then reminded the hotel owner that he was working for the Office of Public Roads, doing pathfinding work, and if the town ever wanted to see a road pass down its main street, he would remove the photos that very minute.

"I was quite surprised when this had no

effect on him whatsoever. So I went on to say I knew the governor of the territory personally, would in fact be seeing him in only a few days time, and I would be sure to tell him about this blight on the good reputation of his territory."

"Did that get his attention?" asked Mr. Thompson.

"One would think so, Mr. Thompson, one would think so. Yet I was surprised to hear him cuss out the governor, calling him a Republican bagman, and if I knew what was good for me, I would leave right then before he went and got his rifle."

Again, we had a hard time not laughing. Mr. Thompson seemed to be holding his stomach as if in pain. As for myself, I couldn't understand why Mr. Westgard did not just return to his room and forget about it. No one was forcing him to stay in the saloon.

"I do not think the man took me seriously,"

Mr. Westgard continued, "so I did indeed speak to the governor in three days time and I made sure to tell him about those photographs on public display in a hotel in his territory, news that seemed to distress him as much as it did me."

He stopped talking after that, a self-satisfied look on his face. Several minutes passed, and we were left wondering if that was the end of the story. Mr. Thompson finally had to ask:

"So what happened?"

"Well, of course the governor heeded my complaint, Mr. Thompson. A few years later, I was told the photos had indeed been removed, a betterment of that territory for which I take no small amount of credit."

A few years later? This time I had to bite my tongue to keep from laughing. Yes, Kansas City would have been Mr. Westgard's kind of town.

center

Sharing the Road with Cannonball Baker

We left Kansas City on the morning of June 20 after Mr. Thompson had sent his obligatory telegrams, I had purchased more gasoline and oil, and Will Foster had spent most of one day travelling back and forth on an electric streetcar, something we allowed him to do after first ensuring he knew the address of the Savoy Hotel. Mr. Thompson paid him when we first arrived in the city although how much money he was able to bring home to his father, I wouldn't want to hazard a guess as he had many parcels with him—toys for the most part—when we dropped him off at the train station.

When we were back on the road, Mr. Thompson spent the first hour going through his trip journal, making pencil calculations and obviously concentrating hard on something. When he finally put down his pencil he looked at the journal as though it were something wonderful, then he said:

"George, do you have any idea what sort of time we made from Pueblo?"

"We made good time," I answered, "I know that. Things certainly speed up when you don't have to use any wood."

"They certainly do. According to the trip log, we were on the road for sixty-two hours. That's running time. In that time, we travelled 702 miles. Do you know what that works out to as our average travelling speed?"

I did the math in my head.

"A little over eleven miles an hour."

"Eleven point three to be exact, George. Our average running speed. Not our fastest speed. Our average speed."

"That's pretty good."

"George, that's bloody amazing. For a fully loaded truck, an eight-and-a-half-ton truck, that's the sort of speed that will get people's attention."

He fell silent for a minute, and I could tell he was thinking about something. When he finally spoke, he said:

"George, my father wants to print pamphlets when our journey is done. Some new sales pamphlets that will tell everyone how well the Pioneer Freighter performed."

"Makes sense."

center

144

CANNONBALL BAKER WITH HIS BELOVED INDIAN MOTORCYCLE.

"Now, I think we have a pretty persuasive case for our truck being as tough as all get out. If we didn't prove that in New Mexico and Arizona, we certainly proved it when we fell through that bridge in Hutchinson, would you agree?"

"I would."

"Now, wouldn't it be beneficial, as well as letting people know how tough the Pioneer Freighter is, if we could also tell them how fast she is? If we showed them that a commercial dray is no competition for a truck. Wouldn't that be a good thing for my father to include in the pamphlets?"

I agreed, and with that, Mr. Thompson started rummaging around in his satchel looking for something, getting more and more excited until finally he withdrew a well-worn map and spread it out on his lap.

"Look at this map, George. This hasn't happened to us before. Look—we are here. And here is Chicago. Do you see it?"

I looked at the map and saw right away what he was talking about. Our route to Chicago consisted pretty much of two straight lines—one straight north to Des Moines, then one straight east to Chicago.

"The land is flat, the course is direct. Do

you know what we should do, George?"

"I'm guessing you want me to push down on the gas pedal."

"George, I want you to push down on that gas pedal as hard as you've ever pushed on anything in your life. Let's have some fun."

For the next 900 miles, the Pioneer Freighter was one of the fastest vehicles on the road, something I don't think many trucks can ever claim. Touring cars pulled over to let us pass. Cars coming in the opposite direction also pulled over in surprise or fear, I couldn't quite decide. We must have looked quite the sight, the truck decked out like a Prairie Schooner, running mad across the land as if it were being chased by the devil himself.

As we barreled down the road, I remembered how painfully slow the travelling had been through New Mexico and Arizona, how on some days we could travel no more than a mile through the mud and the snow, never getting the Pioneer Freighter out of first gear. Or on other days, how we would be rescued by bemused farmers who wanted money for the "short-term rental" of their mules.

I wished I could have seen those farmers now. Seen their faces when we rushed by and left their mules swishing their tails to clear away our dust.

"How cams't thou in that pickle?" I would have yelled as we passed. "How cams't thou . . ." and that's all they would have heard

because by then we would have been a quarter mile down the road.

We sped our way to Des Moines, then Dixon, and I think in the days we spent getting to Chicago, there was only one person who actually passed us, a slight man driving an Indian Motorcycle.

He passed us good and proper, too, a hundred feet to the side, the bike bouncing over the rough farm land of Illinois, not crowding us and risking an accident on the road. When he cut back on the road, he gave us a wave, then a thumbs-up sign before finding another gear on his bike and shooting ahead like a rock fired from a sling shot. Both Mr. Thompson and I stared at him with our mouths agape. Finally, Mr. Thompson closed his mouth and said:

"How fast do you think he was going, George?"

"I wouldn't even want to guess."

"The man could certainly drive a motorcycle. Did you see how smoothly he went off and on the road?"

"I did."

"I wonder who in the world that was."

A few years later, I started seeing photos in the automobile magazines of a slight man sitting on an Indian Motorcycle, always with a bemused smile on his face and a peaked cap on his head. I can't say with certainty that's who we saw that day, but the timing was about right. He had been at the Indianapolis

Speedway the month before. Could still have been in the area on his way to Chicago or New York. The man was always on the road in the United States somewhere.

In a few years, I convinced myself it must have been him because I couldn't think of anyone else who could have passed us that easily, who could have given us a wave and a thumbs-up while controlling his motorcycle with only one hand. Yes, it must have been Cannonball Baker.

I read about the man for years because he was always on some sort of crazy trip, always trying to set some sort of speed record. He could even set records on how quickly he could get a speeding ticket, appear before a judge, and be back on the road.

His real name was Erwin Baker, and he was another Hoosier, born on a farm in Lawrenceburg, Indiana, in 1882. At the age of twelve, he left home and moved to Indianapolis, where he apprenticed as a machinist. He worked in a machine shop for eight years before leaving to join the circus.

You don't run across many man-runs-away-to-join-the-circus stories in life, but Baker had one. Turns out in the years when he was becoming a machinist, he was also trying to become a boxer, a tough task for such a diminutive man, but he could work the speed bag. That was his circus act, standing on a wooden stage hitting the punching bags, run-ning from bag to bag, getting eleven of them gyrating and popping at the same time.

Then, in 1904, he found something that went faster than his punching bags—an Indian Motorcycle. He won his first motor-cycle race that same year, a dirt-track event in Crawfordsville, Indiana. Five years later, he was at the opening of the Indianapolis Motor Speedway, scheduled as a weekend-long event although the later races were cancelled after those five people were killed.

If Baker had any qualms about his cho-sen vocation after that disastrous weekend, they never showed. He kept racing. By 1914, he was in San Diego, looking for something to do, when it occurred to him he might be able to set a transcontinental, motorcycle speed record. He was a smart man, Baker was, because before starting his trip, he checked weather reports for the previous ten years and calculated when the best of time of year would be to drive the bike across the United States to avoid rain and the inevitable mudholes rain would make on the dirt roads (turned out to be early May).

He also arranged for gasoline to be waiting for him at remote points along the way. And meals. He even contacted the state police in Indi-ana to ask a little favour of them—"What will you be needing, Erwin?" the cops asked—and on the day he crossed Indiana, the speed limit in the state was raised to sixty miles per hour. It was lowered again the next day.

He reached New York City in eleven days, twelve hours, and ten minutes, almost twice as fast as the previous record of twenty days, nine hours, and one minute. That trip also gave him his nickname after a reporter with the *New York Tribune* saw the Indian tearing down the macadamized roads of the state and wrote that Baker was faster on his bike than "the Cannon Ball train of the Illinois, Central." Within a few years, people forgot he was ever called Erwin.

That transcontinental run also brought him to the attention of Harry Stutz, who had started the Stutz Motor Company of Indianapolis in 1912. Stutz contacted the hometown hero in late 1914 and asked him: "Cannonball, can you be as crazy on four wheels as you are on two?"

Then Stutz told him he wanted Baker to pilot one of his Bearcat-model cars from San Diego to New York, wanted his company to claim the transcontinental speed record for an automobile, to which request Baker responded:

"And what is the transcontinental record for an automobile, Mr. Stutz?"

"I have no idea," he replied, "nor does it matter. Whatever the last claim was, my car can beat it. I'll furnish the car, you drive it and break the record, and the car is yours."

So Baker agreed. He left San Diego in a modified Bearcat Stutz on May 7, 1915, according to news reports, in front of a crowd so large police had to be called out to control it. In just two days, he was in El Paso, Texas, a distance of 1,000 miles away. News wires reported his progress to an amazed nation, which couldn't imagine anyone travelling that fast.

He raced a train in southern New Mexico, crashed through a barbed wire fence at forty miles an hour in Texas, got lost in the desert, ran out of gas, and still managed to reach New York City on May 18. He had travelled 3,728.4 miles in eleven days, seven hours, and fifteen minutes. This time, Baker was three times faster than the previous record holder.

Overnight, Baker became a national hero. President Woodrow Wilson sent him a congratulatory telegram. Carl Fisher asked him to join the Lincoln Highway Association. Car manufacturers began competing with each other to hire him as a driver for their newest cars.

Baker thanked the president, said no to Fisher and yes to just about every car manufacturer. He wanted to drive—needed to drive it seemed—and over the next twenty years, his trips made him so famous he was eventually listed in the Indianapolis phone directory as Cannonball Baker, because it seemed pointless to use his given name (his wife was the last person on the planet still calling him Erwin).

The very next year, in 1916, Baker drove a Cadillac 8 Roadster from Los Angeles to Times Square in seven days, eleven hours, and fifty-two minutes. Coast to coast in a week. He might have done it faster if not for a speeding ticket in Collinsville, Illinois, where he was pulled over by a motorcycle cop, who said Baker had been travelling at the excessive speed of thirty-two miles per hour.

He was taken to the local police station where a crowd quickly gathered after hearing Cannonball Baker had just been arrested. Baker told the police chief he wished to plead guilty to the offence, and the chief summoned the local judge, who was having lunch at a nearby restaurant. The judge told Baker the fine for driving at such a dangerous speed ranged between five dollars and one hundred dollars. There would also be court costs of three dollars and sixty cents. As Baker waited anxiously for the verdict, the judge told him he owed the township eight dollars and sixty cents.

Baker paid the fine, signed autographs for the crowd, then jumped back behind the wheel of his car. The elapsed time between arrest, conviction, and back on the road was twenty minutes.

Although his transcontinental jaunts of 1915 and 1916 made him a household name, some of his more memorable trips were still to come. In 1926, he drove a loaded, two-ton truck from New York to San Francisco in five days, seventeen hours, and thirty minutes. In 1928, he beat the 20th Century Limited train from New York to Chicago. Then, in 1933, he found another gear. Managed to make speed something volcanic, something that baffled you and couldn't be explained — not by natural laws, not by rational thought, not by past experience.

In that year, he drove a Graham-Paige Blue Streak 8 from New York City to Los Angeles. What happened on that trip is a testament, surely, to the success of the Good Roads Movement, for no rutted or muddy road could have allowed for the speeds Baker hit. It was also a testament to the Blue Streak 8, which was the first car to have enclosed fenders. The first to move the radiator cap under the hood. And fast, brother, that car was fast.

Cannonball Baker took the Blue Streak 8 across America in fifty-three-and-a-half hours. It was a record that stood for forty years. In the middle of the Great Depression, the story of Cannonball Baker and the Blue Streak 8 cheered people right up, made their own plight seem more manageable somehow, let them know that tomorrow didn't have to be like today.

Mr. Thompson Sees His Father

We pulled into Chicago on June 28, and there were all sorts of Saurer people waiting to greet us, including Mr. Thompson's father, whom I had never met before. There were businessmen who owned the Saurer distribution rights for Illinois and Iowa and some people from the head office in New York, including my old boss Mr. Otto. There was even a foreman from the manufacturing factory in Plainfield, New Jersey, who had come to inspect the truck, even though Mr. Thompson had sent him a telegram that the truck was holding up admirably and looked quite capable of completing the journey.

They met us at the front steps of the Palmer House Hotel, where I parked the truck on State Street before taking it to a nearby garage. I stood aside as the men posed for photographs in front of the truck. I don't think the Pioneer Freighter could have looked more out of place—like a motorized covered wagon, dirty and muddy, perhaps still showing some of the red clay from the Wild West—parked there on State Street, surrounded by tall brick buildings and men in dark, three-piece suits.

The men were cheerful and slapped each other on the back many times. I heard one man say, "I never doubted she would make it, not for a minute," although these were the same men who decided to start the trip in Denver just in case we failed. Just in case the truck couldn't make it.

I felt a bit sorry for the truck, which surprised me because it was a machine, and I had never felt any way at all about a machine. But I felt it was being treated unkindly. As if it were being lied to, like a girl on a date that was going badly, but the man didn't have the gumption to tell her, even though she suspected it. There was something fancy and deceitful about the whole welcoming party in Chicago.

I felt relieved when the photographer left, and the men started drifting into the hotel. I jumped quickly behind the wheel and started the magneto ignition, the engine coming to life right away. Before driving away, I saw Mr. Thompson's father pull him aside and draw a piece of paper from his pocket. Heard him say:

"Son, exactly what kind of bridge was this?"

Making Our Way to New York City

We left Chicago on June 30, and the Pioneer Freighter probably could have taken us to New York City in two weeks—maybe even ten days at the speed we were travelling—but it took us another month to get there.

It was strange, this last part of the journey, because it was so different from what we had gone through until then. We crashed through no more bridges. Never had to lay down another corduroy road. Even the weather, if it turned bad, was never a bother again because the roads were macadamized, and we never had to use our camping equipment. There was always a hotel bed to sleep in. A garage to sell us gasoline and oil. A diner to sell us fresh meals. On many days, I felt like a robber baron travelling in his private railcar in the lap of luxury compared to what we had gone through in New Mexico and Arizona.

All these changes meant we should have been making good time, but we couldn't go fast, either. Mr. Thompson had the trip logs to show how fast the Pioneer Freighter had been from Pueblo to Chicago, all the material he and his father needed for the sales pamphlets they would get printed that autumn. As badly as I wanted to push my foot to the gas pedal, to feel that excitement again of making really good time down a decent road, Mr. Thompson said we couldn't.

"I'm afraid we have business we need to attend to, George," and then he told me his father had left strict instructions for us to drive slow: "Go meandering" as he put it, so men could gawk at us when we passed them, could call out for their wives to come to the front porch and watch us pass, our Saurer Ocean-to-Ocean sign brandished proudly on the canvas tarps of the truck.

This part of the trip was all about sales or future sales, and Mr. Thompson plotted a zig-zagging course for us that had the truck going north-south as often as she went west-east. We went to Ypsilanti and Hartford, Cleveland, and Detroit, visited states we didn't need to travel through, and towns where we would spend several nights simply because there was a man living there that Mr. Thompson senior hoped to do business with one day.

We would reach these towns, and Mr.

Thompson always had an address we needed to find for a car-manufacturing factory or one of those new car dealerships, some of them with a display room where the truck would be put behind plate-glass windows. Mr. Thompson would then have to spend a day or two behind the glass, walking around with pamphlets in his hand, waiting for people to come up and talk to him. I would normally stay for an hour or so after getting the truck into position then have the rest of the day to do not much of anything at all.

After a couple of weeks of this, I noticed that Mr. Thompson had worked his sales pitch to a fine art, bowing his head slightly when he handed out a pamphlet and saying "for your consideration." These pamphlets were never crumbled and shoved into a miner's pockets, but the more towns we visited, the more I found myself feeling out of sorts. I missed the mad scamper through the mining camps with gritty Ukrainians singing polkas in the back of the truck. Missed our cook fires. The mountains. The rivers you needed to ford, instead of waiting your turn to cross a toll bridge.

For many of these days, we travelled beside the Great Lakes—Michigan, Ontario, Erie—and I would spy steamers and freighters making their way to distant cities. I imagined the deckhands and the stokers working on those ships, and it seemed a more honest day's work than what I was now doing. I found myself wondering what it would be like to work on a tramp freighter or in a coal mine or out at a cattle ranch.

Maybe the fact that my job was going to be over when we reached New York, while Mr. Thompson would be returning home, had something to do with my mood. I was going to be out of work. No more travelling. No more time on the road. But seeing this country left me wanting to see more of it, not return home to Campbell's Bay where I would have no other job options but to head out to the lumber camps and join the boys I went to school with.

Mr. Thompson seemed to pick up on my blue mood because several times he said: "It's not my call, George, all these sales demonstrations. My father says it needs to be done. I wish we were travelling across the country, too."

"I miss it, you know."

"I miss it, too, George. But we have to make sure we don't get too blue. You can't sell anything if you're blue."

"I'm not blue. I feel fine," I said, denying how I was feeling, remembering how my father once told me nobody really wants to hear the truth anyway. "Anyone asks how you're doing, George, you always tell him you're doing fine. People have enough problems without hearing about yours." That's probably twice as true on a road trip.

So I kept driving—Cleveland, Pittsburgh, Buffalo—wondering from time to time what Mr. Westgard was doing. Mr. Thompson told me one day, he was already organizing

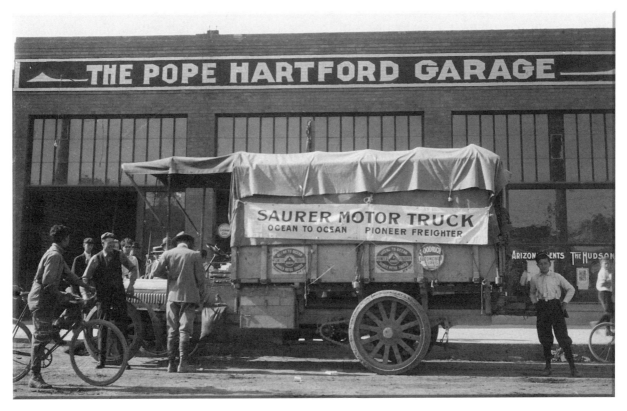

**PEOPLE POSE FOR PHOTOS WITH THE PIONEER FREIGHTER OUTSIDE
AN AUTOMOBILE DEALERSHIP IN HARTFORD, CONNECTICUT.**

another transcontinental journey, this time for the Garford Automobile Company, which would be taking a convoy of paying customers across the United States, following the same route we had just travelled. This would be another first for the man. Until then, no one had ever paid to be a passenger on a road trip across the States. Before that trip, if you were taking a horseless carriage across the United States, you either owned a car or were a pathfinder like Mr. Westgard.

People paying to go on a road trip. At first the notion seemed crazy to me. The closer we got to New York City, the less crazy it seemed.

I read about the Garford road trip later that year; how it had been organized by a tour company out of New York City, the Raymond and Whitcomb Company, which had been organizing automobile tours through New England for several years. Passengers paid 875 dollars to go on what the tour company called the "first transcontinental automobile train." That wasn't a cheap fare as 800 dollars would buy you a Model T, and you could drive it for years, not just ride around for a month or two.

I gather other people must have felt the same way because there were only five cars in the "automobile train," not counting Mr. Westgard, who drove in a lead car with his wife and the man who owned the Raymond and Whitcomb Company. I don't really see how they could have made money, but maybe they were hoping for future business because they went ahead anyway.

The tourists left New York City on October 2 after first posing for photos in front of Grant's Tomb on the Hudson River. I saw that photo later. All the cars had numbers on them like racing cars, and there were several women in the party, some of them dressed in fur coats.

The tour company said the party would travel on a fixed schedule and promised only two nights of outdoor camping, the schedule bringing them to hotels and inns every other night. On the two nights of camping, for those who didn't want to sleep outside, Raymond and Whitcomb had even arranged to stop near a rail line where a Pullman sleeping car would be waiting.

I don't know how long the fur coats lasted because the automobile train soon encountered a lot of the same problems we did—snowstorms in the Rockies, quicksand in New Mexico, wild temperature swings in Arizona, so the wheels of the cars froze in mud. They may have even been a bit unluckier than us because they hit rain in Kansas, which turned the Great Plains into a mud field. One news story I read quoted Mr. Westgard calling it "gumbo mud."

He did a good job keeping the party on schedule, though. The automobile train arrived in San Diego on November 22 and was in Los Angeles the following day, exactly as the fixed schedule said it would be. The tour company arranged for a parade to be held in Los Angeles to welcome the passengers into the city. Several of them then boarded ships to continue their holidays in the Orient.

It was funny reading the sales brochures that came out after that trip, the tour company discounting all the hardships they encountered. It said the women passengers, in particular, enjoyed the journey because of the "beneficial exercise." I knew what that meant. Pushing a car out of the mud.

Still, I had to admire Mr. Westgard for pulling it off. Keeping to a fixed schedule down the Trail to Sunset. Things were starting to get easier almost month by month.

End of a Road Trip

On August 1, we reached White Plains, New York where we spent the night in an inn. Mr. Thompson treated me to a fine meal that night, complete with red wine and a selection of cakes for dessert. We spent most of the meal talking about our road trip, which would finish the next day.

"Did you ever doubt we would make it, George?"

"Plenty of times," I answered. "When you first saw Indian Slough, didn't you think we were in trouble?"

"Quite a pickle. How cams't thou in that pickle? I'm surprised Mr. Westgard didn't start yelling that as soon as we saw it."

"He was too busy swimming."

"And that horrid little bridge in Kansas. My father had to pay most of the cost from his own pocket. His partners in New York said we should have found a different route."

"I didn't see another bridge, did you?"

"No. I didn't see much of a bridge after we left, either."

I laughed at that. It was a funny thing to remember, that bridge collapsing; and why we weren't killed that day was still a mystery to me. I had had bad dreams quite a few nights after, imagining my body lying on the shores of the Arkansas River, people standing over me and saying what a fool I'd been, what a fool thing it had been, trying to drive a truck across the United States of America.

"But we did it, George. Busted bridges, snowstorms, the White Mountains. We made it through everything. My father is quite pleased. He sent a telegram last night admitting he had doubts we could pull it off. Wasn't sure we were going to get the truck to New York City after Mr. Westgard left."

"He thought we were too young?"

"I gather he did. He told me the Saurer men in New York tried to convince Mr. Westgard to stay with us, but he told them he had other commitments."

"Maybe he'll be at city hall tomorrow to greet us."

"Father says he is already doing some work for the Triple A. I don't know if it's started yet, but apparently he's taking a car to Florida. He may not even be in the city."

"Taking a car to Florida?"

"That's what I'm told."

I was bewildered by this answer and without realizing what I was doing — saying pretty near the same thing I uttered when Mr. Westgard told me I would be driving a truck from Denver to Los Angeles — I said:

"Are there roads to Florida?"

"Probably not, George. Although after what we have done this summer, I think the roads will be coming. Father says it will be a new world soon."

The next morning, I awoke to the loud bleeping of horns and combustible engines. The Motor Truck Club of New York had arrived to be our escort into the city. In the lead car was Mr. Thompson's father, who had arrived by train from Chicago the night before.

"So you boys made it," he said when we had come downstairs. "Come, we have to get moving. I have arranged a proper reception for us."

We had a hurried breakfast then climbed into the Pioneer Freighter for the short drive into Manhattan. Mr. Thompson's father, who was dressed in heavy tweeds and had a jaunty-looking boating hat perched upon his head, sat beside me while his son sat on some planks of wood in the bed of the truck in pretty much the same position he had been sitting when we left Denver five months earlier. Mr. Thompson junior didn't seem to mind, though, and kept smiling at everything his father said.

We drove over the Macomb's Dam Bridge, the Harlem River below us already starting to refract the early morning sun, the rolling waves throwing the light in a straight line down the river. It was a clear day, and as I looked behind me, I could just make out the shadowy outline of the Catskill Mountains. In front of us was the skyline of Manhattan.

There were about a dozen trucks escorting us, and together we took over the bridge, the trucks driving in front, beside, and behind us, everyone in a jovial mood, until we crossed the bridge and started making our way down 155th Street. At that point, the trucks fell into a straight horizontal line, Mr. Thompson's father yelling that no one could see the Ocean-to-Ocean sign if everyone drove beside us.

People stared at us as we made our way down the street, but there was not the finger pointing we got out West or even in some of the towns in Illinois and Michigan. New York City had been hosting transcontinental horse-less carriage parties for nearly a decade now, and anyway, it was New York. People rarely pointed at anything here.

We made our way down 155th Street and turned onto Broadway, making our way slowly past the theatres with their long awnings and carpets laid out right on the sidewalk. Mr. Thompson's father told us breathlessly that when we reached city hall there would be other Saurer types waiting for us, some borough politicians he had lined up, perhaps

GETTING AN ESCORT INTO NEW YORK CITY

even the mayor although this was not certain.

The truck was running smoothly, and as we drove, I found myself patting the side of my door as if the truck were a hunting dog that had just performed well. Again, I was not accustomed to having any feelings at all toward a machine and I put my hand back on the steering wheel when I realized what I was doing.

The trucks parading us down the street kept honking their horns, some of the passengers breaking into a song I had never heard with lines about an open road and the glory of John McAdam. People continued to stop and stare at us as we passed while others ran across the street before we came so they wouldn't have to wait; those folks seemed somewhat annoyed when they looked back.

When we reached city hall, the mayor was indeed waiting for us. The sight of William J. Gaynor made Mr. Thompson's father sit straight in his seat.

"See, son, the mayor is here as well," he said. "We have done well, my boy, we have done well."

I wondered for a second what exactly Mr. Thompson's father had done other than give us the truck. It seemed like taking credit for winning a hockey game if you brought the puck. But I said nothing, just pulled in front of city hall as the mayor came walking down the steps to greet us. Some other men dressed in similar black suits walked behind him. Mr. Thompson's father almost tripped, he got out of the truck so fast.

The mayor shook all our hands and complimented Mr. Thompson's father on reaching New York City. He went on to talk about the growing importance of "motorized cargo vehicles," and how they would add to the economic prosperity of his city; how he was glad the Saurer Motor Truck Company had chosen New York City for its corporate headquarters instead of some "little town in Michigan."

After that, the mayor posed for photographs with Mr. Thompson's father; the other men with him took turns standing in front of the camera. The entire affair took more than an hour, the members of the Motor Truck Club of New York City also wanting to pose in front of the truck before the photographer left.

When this was finished, the mayor walked back up the steps of city hall, most of the men following him, including Mr. Thompson's father and most of the Saurer executives. Mr. Thompson shook my hand and said he needed to go as well, but promised to see me the next day when his business was concluded.

"Can you look after my satchel, George?" he asked. "Father has brought city clothes for me." And with that, he ran up the steps.

I drove the truck back down Broadway to a garage on 55th Street. I started stripping the truck, taking down the canvas tarps, the Ocean-to-Ocean sign, the wooden planks that had made up the bed of the truck. It was tedious work, but I had nothing else to do that day and didn't mind.

Mr. Thompson and his father caught a train to Chicago late the following day but not before treating me to lunch at the outdoor restaurant on top of Madison Square Gardens. Mr. Thompson's father told us that there had been a truck exposition in the Gardens in early January of that very year, the first of its kind in the United States. More than 200 trucks had been on display, which told us, he said, "where things are heading boys. If I owned any railway stock I would be getting rid of it now." I didn't own any railway stock but thanked him for his good advice.

The Thompsons took a motorized cab to Grand Central Station after that, and I never saw Mr. Thompson again although he encouraged me to visit if I ever made my way back to Chicago.

"It would be lovely to see you, George," he said. "My father may even be able to find work for you if you are in the market."

I told him that was a nice offer but not

**GEORGE MACLEAN, WITH A STRIPPED-DOWN TRUCK ON THE
STREETS OF NEW YORK CITY, AUGUST, 1911.**

Barbara Arnott

necessary. I had a few prospects I wanted to pursue. Some ideas that had come to me the last few days on the road. He told me he was glad to hear it. Mr. Thompson's father then told me that the foreman from the Saurer plant in Plainfield would be at the garage the next morning to take carriage of the truck.

On the way back to the hotel, I stopped at the garage to see the truck one more time. It looked strange, stripped of all its canvas and wood, like some hardwood tree in the middle of winter. Figuring no one would mind if I drove it out of the garage, I went for a quick tour around Manhattan.

I passed the Fuller Building and marvelled again at the size of it, so tall people had started to call it a skyscraper, and the new public library building on Fifth Avenue, which had opened earlier that summer. I read in a newspaper that there were more than one million books inside that building and couldn't imagine such a thing. After a while, I found myself back in front of city hall where I thought I saw the mayor hurry down the steps and jump into a waiting cab. Perhaps it was because I had stripped the truck, but he didn't seem to recognize me.

On my way back to the garage, I saw one of those street photographers carrying a portable Kodak, the ones who loitered on Broad-way Avenue looking for tourists who might want to have their photograph taken. I asked him how much he charged for a photo, and he told me two bits. I gave him the coins, slicked down my hair, and sat up straight behind the wheel of the truck.

I picked up the photo the next day at his shop on 42nd Street. I mailed it to my mother in Campbell's Bay, who framed it and told everyone what I had done. She told me most people agreed it was a nice photo although no one really believed the story.

Albuquerque Morning Journal

ALBUQUERQUE, NEW MEXICO, TUESDAY, MAY 30, 1911

WESTGARD LOSES FIFTEEN POUNDS

Pilot of Motor Truck Says He Would Not Repeat
Back-breaking Trip for $10,000

NEW YORK, N-Y, MAY 27 — A.L. Westgard, president of the Touring Club of America arrived in New York City on the 22nd, having come directly from Los Angeles after completing the first leg of the "ocean to ocean" trip of the five-ton Saurer truck which is carrying three-and-a-half ton cargo from Denver to New York via San Francisco. . .

Mr. Westgard in addition to undertaking the long journey to demonstrate the practicability of a commercial car for any conditions of road or weather bore a commission from the national government to plot the most practicable routes for the establishment of highways for the transportation of troops and munitions of war in the event of future hostilities.

In an interview shortly after getting back to New York Mr. Westgard had the following to say: "Not for 10,000 dollars would I repeat that awful, nerve-racking, black breaking punishment again. The pictures which we made of the hardships we went through tell the story graphically and I can assure you that these pictures do not represent exceptional conditions but average every day conditions, not hardships for a few minutes of a day but in many instances for the whole day and day after day. Not once in the 68 days of grilling punishment did we have even moderately easy going. We were constantly digging the big truck out of the bottomless mires, which only the axles prevented from sinking further, or planking the road continually with lumber from our cargo to secure traction sufficiently to creep along at a snail's pace . . .

"I can truthfully say that never in my life have I seen the brutality of the punishment we had to give the big truck duplicated in the history of any machine. It was a test of the endurance of metal and of men, which stands unparalleled in the annals of self-propelled vehicles."

A.L. WESTGARD, 1911.

Barbara Arnott

Epilogue

Trucking — The Next 100 Years

Two weeks after George MacLean and Arthur Thompson arrived in New York City, a dusty Packard panel truck made its way down Sunset Boulevard in Los Angeles. The Packard had left New York City on July 12 and, by taking a different route, had completed a continuous, transcontinental run in thirty-two days. The Pioneer Freighter may have been the first truck to drive across the United States, but it was almost a lucky thing it set off when it did. No truck, ever again, would take five months to complete the journey.

By 1926, the record for a transcontinental truck run was held by Cannonball Baker — five days, seventeen hours, and thirty minutes. Five months winnowed down to five days. The improvements made to the motorized cargo vehicle in just fifteen years — the changes that took place in America during the same time — were nothing short of remarkable.

The apex of horse and mule ownership in the United States came in 1918. In that year, there were an estimated 27 million horses and mules in the United States. That number would decrease, at an annual shrinkage rate of 2 percent, for the next thirty years, bottoming out at just under 11.5 million.

There was a collateral increase in automobile and truck ownership. In 1918, there were an estimated 7 million cars and trucks on the road in the United States. Within eleven years, the figure was 29 million. In 1918, one in thirteen families had a car or truck. By 1929, it was four out of five.

America had fallen in love with the horseless carriage. In particular, she had fallen head over heels in love with the combustible-engine style of a horseless carriage. While electric cars were the top-selling cars in America in 1900, by 1918 they were virtually extinct and would remain so until the turn of the century.

Steam-engine cars and trucks would suffer a similar fate. While several of the steam-engine companies could boast of better performance and more racing records than their combustible-engine cousins — the White Motor Company of Cleveland, Ohio, with its celebrated White Steamer, won many of America's prestigious races between 1900 and 1910, including the Los Angeles-to-Phoenix Road Race of 1909 — the American public was enthralled with the new technology of combustible-engine motors.

By the start of the roaring '20s, it was hard to find an electric- or steam-engine motor company still operating in the United States. America had chosen a destination—a direction—that it would stay with for the next eighty years.

Shortly after the Pioneer Freighter arrived in New York City, it began to dawn on America's railway companies that they may have made a strategic blunder by supporting the Good Roads Movement.

This "what-have-we-done" feeling grew stronger the next year when Carl Fisher founded the Lincoln Highway Association and stronger still when membership in the American Automobile Association started growing by leaps and bounds.

Suddenly, this little oddity called the horseless carriage—which was only supposed to transport people and freight to the nearest railway siding—was a legitimate threat. For the next decade, the railway companies fought any plan to have the federal government set aside funds for the construction of new roads or to play any role in the transportation industry.

Any and all arguments were brought to bear by the railway companies: The American military could not entrust the nation's security to motorized cargo vehicles. The American government should not spend money enriching the profit sheets of men like Carl Fisher, Henry Ford, Billy Durant, or Alexander Winton. The railway companies even argued that the nation's prosperity was dependent on their

well being. Why, a downturn in rail business could throw the entire country into recession.

It was a fierce fight, but by 1921 the railway companies had lost. That year, the federal government passed the Federal Aid Highway Act, which committed federal funds to the building and maintaining of a national road system.

If the passage of the Federal Aid Highway Act of 1921 ended the argument between the railway companies and the motor companies, it also spelled the end of the Good Roads Movement. The various Good Roads committees and chapters—combined, they were the largest public-interest group in the United States at the turn of the last century—suddenly found there was no war left to wage.

Most of the leaders of the movement went on to other pursuits. Carl Fisher started building Miami Beach. Horatio—"Good Roads"—Earle ran unsuccessfully for the Republican gubernatorial nomination in Michigan. Some local chapters continued the fight for state funds, among them Kansas and New Mexico, but even these chapters were closed by the end of the decade.

The most lasting monument to the movement—aside from the actual roads—is the American Automobile Association, which, instead of fading away after 1921, grew more influential as the only national advocacy group for America's burgeoning number of motorists.

The AAA went on to pioneer the road map

(its first was A.L. Westgard's *Trail to Sunset*), driver safety, and group auto insurance. The AAA now has affiliated clubs in every state in America and more than 55 million members.

As for the early pioneers of the motor age and the Good Roads Movement, it was a yin-yang fate that awaited them. Some were caught in the rush of the times and landed safely years down the road, rich and famous beyond their wildest dreams. Others crashed and burned.

Henry Ford, whose first two automotive companies went bankrupt, went on to become one of the wealthiest and most powerful businessmen in America. His Model T car and refinement of the Chicago slaughterhouse disassembly line revolutionized the automotive industry. He died at the age of eighty-three in his Dearborn, Michigan, mansion.

His archrival at the turn of the last century, Alexander Winton, was a crash-and-burn victim. The Winton Motor Carriage Company was one of the first car manufacturers in the United States, and it was a Winton Touring Car that made the first transcontinental automobile trip in 1903.

Winton built luxury cars—handcrafted, beautiful cars—his company once stiff competition for manufacturers like Cadillac, Packard, and Peerless. He held more than one hundred automotive patents; gave Henry Ford his steering-wheel-assembly design because he said it was "unsafe" for any car not to have

it. However, he never adjusted to Ford's mass production, and his company ran into financial problems in the early '20s. It went out of business in 1924. Alexander Winton died eight years later.

Go through the early annals of motoring in the United States, and the facts go back and forth like that as steady as a metronome. For every winner, there is a loser. For every success story, there is a sad tale of promise dashed. Jack Mack's story provides a good example of the cruel, ironic fate in store for many of these men.

The first American to build trucks, and nothing but trucks, Mack stormed out of the company J.P. Morgan formed between the Mack brothers and Saurer, promising that he would show the New York financier how to run a truck company. He would simply start from scratch and do it again.

It never happened. After parting ways with Morgan, Mack started a new company with a man named Roland Carr, trying to market a line of light trucks. The Mac-Carr Motor Company went bankrupt in less than two years. The partners tried again, this time relocating the company to Allentown, Pennsylvania. Maybe lightning would strike twice. It didn't. This company also went bankrupt.

Mack earned a living after that by selling Republic Trucks; it was a much inferior product to the vehicle that the Mack brothers had built, and which the company that bears his name still manufactures. He was on a sales call for Republic on March 14, 1924, driving outside the town limits of Weatherly, Pennsylvania, when he had his last bit of bad luck.

Somehow a trolley car forced Mack's Chandler Coupe off the road that day, something you wouldn't dare write as fiction for fear no one would believe you—the man who built the first motorized trolley car in the United States killed by a motorized trolley car twenty-four years later. Who would believe a story like that?

But it was a Lehigh Valley Transit Company trolley that forced Jack Mack off the road mid-afternoon on a warm, early spring day, the sun sitting higher in the sky than perhaps you might be accustomed. The trolley forced him to the right, then off the road, then straight into a street post.

Jack Mack died at the age of fifty-nine and is buried in Fairview Cemetery in Allentown, Pennsylvania. His tombstone is shaped like the grill of a Mack truck.

Cannonball Baker fared better. The car companies never stopped looking for his services. He set speed records for four decades and never suffered a serious crash. At the end of every trip, he returned home to Indianapolis to his wife and children, although by 1948 he was starting to slow down—he was sixty-six by then—and accepted a job as the first commissioner of NASCAR. That same year, he set

his last speed record, driving a Nash up the side of Mount Washington in New Hampshire in fifteen minutes, twelve seconds.

Baker passed away at Community Hospital in Indianapolis in 1960 at the age of seventy-eight. After his death, he became a cult hero to many racing enthusiasts who still revere his 53.5-hour cross-country run of 1934. Baker's life and exploits led to no less than five movies, *Cannonball Run*, released in 1981 and starring Burt Reynolds, Roger Moore, Dom DeLuise, and Farrah Fawcett, being the most widely known.

The movie was inspired by the Cannonball Baker Sea-to-Shining-Sea Memorial Trophy Dash, an outlaw race created by *Car and Driver Magazine* that was held four times in the '70s before being disbanded in 1979. The most famous participant of the race was American racing legend Dan Gurney, who won the 24 Hours of Le Mans in 1967. Gurney won the second Cannonball race, held in 1972, while driving a Ferrari Daytona.

While being interviewed by *Car and Driver Magazine* after the race, he made a comment that surely would have brought a smile to the face of Cannonball Baker.

"At no time," said Gurney, "did we exceed 175 miles an hour."

And then there was Carl Fisher. After building the Indianapolis Speedway, spearheading the construction of North America's first coast-to-coast highway, creating Miami Beach from a mango swamp, and amassing a personal fortune of more than 100 million dollars by 1925, he lost everything in the stock market crash of 1929.

He spent the rest of his life doing occasional promotional jobs for his friends and former business partners. He never made more than 500 dollars a month. Lived in an outbuilding on a Vanderbilt estate in south Florida.

The last thing he ever did—and it was a strange endeavour, given this was a man who always wanted the fastest cars, the longest highways, the most expensive homes—was to convince his friends to invest in a small fishing lodge in Key Largo. It was called the Caribbean Club, although Fisher often referred to it as "The Poor Man's Retreat."

Most days after the club opened, you could find Fisher sitting in the bar drinking beer, talking to fishermen about the weather, the day's catch, work, and family. (Fisher's wife left him in 1926. They had no children.) He died in a Miami hospital in 1939 at the age of sixty-five. His pallbearers included Barney Oldfield, Gar Wood, and William Vanderbilt.

Eight years after his death, his ex-wife published a book about Fisher's life. She called it *Fabulous Hoosier*. In it Jane Fisher said of her ex-husband: "He was all speed. I don't believe he ever thought in terms of money. He made millions, but they were incidental. He often said 'I just like to see the dirt fly.'"

Many of the cars and trucks these early pioneers drove have been preserved. The Winton Touring Car that drove across the United States for the first time is in the Smithsonian Institute. One of the first trolley cars built by the Mack brothers is on permanent display at the Mack Trucks Historical Museum in Allentown, Pennsylvania.

Although Saurer published pamphlets for the next two years extolling the Pioneer Freighter and how it performed on what passed for American roads in 1911, it seems the company made no attempt to actually preserve the truck.

All of Saurer's corporate documents became part of the International Motor Company after the merger in 1911 and were eventually handed over to the Mack Trucks Historical Museum. The original Pioneer Freighter pamphlets and many of the photos taken by A.L. Westgard are part of the museum's permanent collection. There is no record, however, of what happened to the truck.

A search at the Detroit Public Library National Automotive History Collection and the Automobile Reference Collection of the Free Library of Philadelphia—the two premier automotive research libraries in the United States—also turns up no record of the Pioneer Freighter.

A similar search at the American Truck Historical Society, the United States Department of Transportation (which has the old records from the Office of Public Roads), the American Automobile Association, and the United States National Archives also draws a blank. The truck simply disappears. Given there was no attempt to promote or preserve the truck, it seems likely it was shipped back to Chicago where it was probably sold. As a Saurer truck could easily rake up a million miles on its odometer (as could a vintage Mack), it may have been on the road somewhere in the Midwest for up to two decades after 1911.

It probably would have been scrapped after that or else ended up in a farmer's barn somewhere. Perhaps it is still out there, rusting somewhere beside an old Harvester tractor (it was, after all, a hard truck to destroy).

Mystery also surrounds one of the men who made the first transcontinental truck run. A similar search through libraries, archives, and government departments gives no hint as to what happened to Arthur Thompson after he returned to Chicago with his father in August of 1911.

It is possible that with the merger of Saurer and Mack one month later, the Thompsons decided to leave the newly formed company. Or perhaps J.P. Morgan had ideas about who should hold the distribution rights for the International Motor Company, and the Thompsons did not fit into those plans.

All that is left of Arthur Thompson are a few telegram dispatches and a handful of photographs taken of him during the journey. We see him as a broad-shouldered, good-looking young man often posed in front of some ridiculous obstacle that A.L. Westgard must have considered worthy of a photo—stuck in the mud of the White Mountains, crashed through a wooden culvert in New Mexico, blocked by a fallen log in California.

You wonder at the young man's stamina and tenacity. You can see in the photos that his clothing is a notch above both George MacLean's and A.L. Westgard's—fine leather boots, a wide-brimmed hat that keeps its shape; many of the photos even show him wearing a tie. He came from a prosperous family. Manual work would have been something new for him.

Yet he was there for every mile of the trip. Without complaint. Without shirking any of the work. You wonder what happened to him after 1911. Did he fight in the Great War? Did he stay in Chicago? Did his journey across the United States give him wanderlust?

Perhaps the questioning is unnecessary, and we simply want to add to a story that is complete. Perhaps Arthur Thompson's destiny in life was simply to accompany George MacLean and Anton Westgard on the first truck trip across the United States. As though nothing more were needed from him. As though this one crazy act were enough.

As for Anton Westgard, there is no shortage of documents showing what he did after 1911.

That same year, he piloted not only the Garford "automobile train" from New York City to San Francisco but also mapped a route from Washington, D.C., to Jacksonville, Florida, for the American Automobile Association.

The next year, he became a permanent field representative for the AAA and made no less than three transcontinental runs for the association. Much of his work in those years was done behind the wheel of the Premier Pathfinder, the car most closely associated with him; you often see it in photographs of the man. The car always had an American flag flying from one of the window struts as well as a brass plaque affixed to the driver's door, letting curious bystanders know that the car was called the "Pathfinder" and that it was piloted by A.L. Westgard, field representative for the American Automobile Association.

A relentless self-promoter, Westgard filed numerous articles and dispatches to newspapers and automotive magazines in the decade that followed the first transcontinental truck trip. He asked reporters, when they interviewed him, to refer to him as a pathfinder and suggested other phrases they could use if they wanted to change it up: Daniel Boone with a Gas Can; the Marco Polo of the Motor Age.

He invented the Skip-Along-Bungalow and often took his second wife, Helen, and his eldest son, James, on his path-finding trips. There is no indication he had many close friends. The only name mentioned in most of Westgard's articles is A.L. Westgard.

The United States Patent Office holds a registered patent that Westgard filed in 1915, an emblem with the initials TCA. This is perhaps in reference to the Touring Club of America, a short-lived motoring club he founded although there is no record the emblem was ever used.

In 1920, he self-published a book called *Tales of a Pathfinder*, a loosely structured recollection of his years on the road. In the book, Westgard dismisses many of his fellow pathfinders, saying they were often deceitful about their exploits, and that he had travelled "more different miles than any other man in the United States." Many of the anecdotes from *Tales of a Pathfinder*—Indian Slough, Fort Apache, the dirty-picture saloon keeper—have been included in this book.

In 1920, he took a leave of absence from the American Automobile Association to accept another government commission, this time to map a route linking national parks in the American West and Southwest. The route he laid out became the National Park-to-Park Highway, connecting twelve national parks in California, Oregon, Washington, Arizona, New Mexico, Colorado, and Utah.

Westgard partially led the first trip on that highway, a seventy-six-day journey he was unable to finish. While making the trip, he became ill and was shipped by train to a hospital in Oakland, California. Discharged a few days later, he decided to spend the winter in California in hopes of speeding along his recovery. He became ill again in early spring and was taken to hospital in San Diego where he passed away on April 13, 1921.

Given what we know of the man, it is hard to understand the cause of his death other than to speculate on whether some sort of madness overtook him one night in his beloved desert—the no-nonsense Norwegian briefly overcome with abandon, letting himself slip away just once, forgetting to count penance, forgetting to forge a path.

Or maybe he was deceitful. Had demons no one knew about, and it was all a pose, this sanctimonious man who once berated an innkeeper for having photos of nude women on display behind his bar.

On the death certificate, doctors listed the cause of death as complications due to syphilis. A.L. Westgard was fifty-five. Westgard Pass in the Inyo Mountains of California is named in his honour.

George MacLean also stayed on the road. His travels over the next ten years are well documented in postcards he mailed to his mother, brother-in-law, and future wife back in Campbell's Bay, Quebec.

He worked for a spell as a miner in Silver City, New Mexico. As a mechanic for the White Motor Company in San Diego. He sent postcards from Utah, Nevada, Colorado, and Michigan. A hard worker, he had no trouble finding work as he crisscrossed the United States. He even continued doing demonstration work for the International Motor Company, driving Mack trucks after a while and thoroughly falling in love with the vehicles.

In 1919, he convinced his childhood sweetheart (a young woman who had the same surname, something George MacLean always thought was a convenient twist of fate) to visit him in California. Margaret MacLean was a traveller herself, a nurse who had worked in Newfoundland and Ontario as well as Quebec. Their postcards had become steadily more intimate over the years, and she agreed to come for a "short visit." They were married the next year.

Friends and family of MacLean describe him as a man of few words, and a prized family possession is the postcard he sent to his brother-in-law shortly after the wedding. Mailed from Catalina Island, MacLean tells his brother-in-law he is spending a couple of days at the seaside resort before returning to Los Angeles, and the weather is fine. Then scrawled along the side of the card as something he almost forgot to mention are the words, "We were married July 22."

The couple's only son, John, was born in California in 1921. Perhaps, with a young family, MacLean decided it was time to go home. He returned to Canada the same year and soon opened an automotive repair shop and garage in Campbell's Bay, the first such business in western Quebec. It is said he built an early prototype of a fully automatic transmission but never got around to patenting it, choosing instead to drop it under the hood of a big, black Buick that he drove around the Ottawa Valley every weekend.

People would tell him every time they saw the car that he was crazy. He should patent a thing like that. When the first mass-produced semi-automatic transmission came off a General Motors assembly line in 1934, someone told MacLean about it. He reportedly shrugged his shoulders and went back to work.

He always loved working on trucks and had a special affinity for Mack. His garage was littered with Mack paraphernalia: bulldog hood ornaments, brochures, chrome lettering. Years after he died, the company gave his widow a Mack pin and certificate in honour of her husband's role in guiding the first truck across the United States. His daughter-in-law, who lives in Peterborough, Ontario, still has the pin. She says it would have been one of MacLean's most prized possessions had he been alive to receive it.

People say MacLean never spoke much about that first truck trip across the United States although that was a surprise to no one who knew him as it wasn't like George MacLean to talk much about anything. Although those who knew the story would ask him questions from time to time, and he always answered politely.

"I guess New Mexico would have been the hardest," he'd say. "Didn't have much in the way of roads at all down there at the time."

Or: "He was a strange little man, Mr. Westgard, but he knew how to get around a car, I'll give him that."

George MacLean died in 1962 at the age of seventy-eight. He is buried in St. Andrew's United Cemetery in Campbell's Bay. Forty-one years after his death, the township erected a stone plaque in his honour, commemorating that historic 1911 trip. In an ironic twist, much of the information on the plaque is wrong. It reads:

George MacLean drove the first self-propelled motorized vehicle (Saurer Motor Truck, now Mack Truck) across North America in 1911. The crew of three left New York City in March and arrived in San Diego, California, in July—a distance of 2,300 miles. The MacLean family home is in the background and his shop stood on this very site.

If he were alive today, the first man to drive a truck across the United States would probably be laughing.

Campbell's Bay, Early 1960s

So what to make of it? I spent a lot of time when I got back home, tinkering around in the garage, trying to come up with a good answer to that question.

It seemed, at the time, we had done something special. It surely did. The cars coming to meet us the other side of the Harlem River, so we could be escorted into Manhattan; all the horns going off like crazy, every motor association and Good Roads person in New York driving behind us, it seemed—I'll never forget that day.

We didn't mind the celebration, either. Didn't shy away from it, the way you do sometimes when people are putting out too much effort. We thought we deserved it. Honestly did. The sand storms in New Mexico, going over the Continental Divide, crashing through that bridge in Kansas. We thought that trip was worth celebrating.

Then a Packard drove out to Los Angeles two weeks later and destroyed our time. Just destroyed it. Thirty-two days, when it had taken us five months. It was embarrassing.

Then all sorts of cars and trucks were making that trip, and within a few years, it seemed a silly boast saying you had driven across the United States in a truck. As though that was some sort of accomplishment. As if people should pat you on the back for doing a thing like that.

I laughed, mind you, when the U.S. military tried to make a similar trip from Washington to San Francisco in the spring of 1919 and bogged down with all the same troubles we had. Eisenhower was with that convoy. They talked about it when he became president; how he had been one of the first to cross the United States in a truck. Like we didn't even exist.

I never saw Mr. Westgard after that trip but I followed what he was doing in the automotive magazines. I read in one of those magazines how he died, and although at first I was surprised to read this, it seemed right to me later that he had been in his automobile when he became ill.

There wasn't much need for pathfinders after that, so it might have been a good thing he went when he did. I don't know what else the man could have done, if you want my honest opinion.

So what did we accomplish? Like I said, I've wondered about that.

The route we took back in 1911 became part of Route 66, and I guess that's something. Even heard a song on the radio the other day called "Route 66," so I gather some people think it's a big deal.

On the other hand, Saurer didn't last very long. If the purpose of our trip was to put that company on the map, you'd have to say we failed

GEORGE MACLEAN IN 1917.
Barbara Arnott

miserably. Mind you, it was going to be hard to compete with Mack, no matter what we did.

I never heard from Mr. Thompson or his father after the trip. Couldn't even follow what they were doing, the way I could with Mr. Westgard. They just disappeared. On my way back to Canada, I stopped in Chicago and tried to track them down but the Saurer display room was long gone, and there were too many Thompsons in the phone book to even start looking.

It felt good coming back home. I don't know whether Mr. Westgard ever had a place he called home, but I realized as soon as I got back to the Ottawa Valley that I had one. My dad had a workshop he let me use, and I opened a garage, so things worked out well.

From time to time, people ask me about the trip, and I always try to answer them as best I can. How tough it was. How it felt to go over the Continental Divide or drive down Broadway Avenue. People seem to like the stories although I never go around looking for ways to tell them.

Lots of people drive cars and trucks now. It seems every second person around here has a pickup. The roads are pretty decent, too. Haven't seen a macadamized road in years. Most everything is paved.

A fellow the other day said I had something to do with that. Said if it weren't for people like me and Mr. Thompson and Mr. Westgard, maybe the Good Roads Movement never would have worked, maybe the government never would have got involved. I told him he was pouring a little something into my ear, but he seemed real serious. He called me a pioneer.

So I don't know, maybe we did do something. I've been working on cars and trucks my whole life. People come in sometimes and tell me they're on a road trip, they just broke down, need the vehicle back as soon as possible. I tell them I know what they're talking about. They're trying to have an adventure. I understand that. Lift the hood and get to work.

About the Author

Ron Corbett is an author, journalist, and broadcaster living in Ottawa. He has won numerous awards for his writing. *A Grand Adventure* is his fifth book. Previous works include *The Last Guide*, which was a Canadian bestseller, and *One Last River Run.*

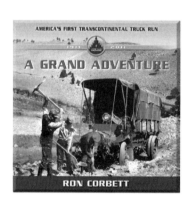

AMERICA'S FIRST TRANSCONTINENTAL TRUCK RUN

A GRAND ADVENTURE

RON CORBETT

TO ORDER MORE COPIES:

GSPH

GENERAL STORE PUBLISHING HOUSE
499 O'Brien Road, Box 415, Renfrew, Ontario, Canada K7V 4A6
Tel 1.800.465.6072 • Fax 1.613.432.7184
www.gsph.com